W9-BBM-267

ROBERT HALLOWELL GARDINER

From a photograph taken about 1860

Early Recollections

OF

Robert Hallowell Gardiner

1782 - 1864

PRINTED FOR
R. H. GARDINER AND W. T. GARDINER
BY
WHITE & HORNE COMPANY
HALLOWELL, MAINE
1936

PREFACE

These memoirs were written seventy-five years ago primarily for the author's children, and with no thought of publication. The chronicle of events ceases about a hundred years ago, when the children were all of an age to remember.

Now, when there are descendants running into the fifth generation, it seems appropriate to have printed copies available; and perhaps a few words of explanation are desirable.

The author was born in 1782 and died in 1864. He was named for his father, Robert Hallowell, and on coming of age in 1803, he added the name of his maternal grandfather, Gardiner, to comply with the terms of the devise to him of the large tract of land in Maine, including what is now the City of Gardiner. There he lived and labored for community, church and state, and there, in his eightieth year, he wrote in his own hand these memoirs.

These were later copied out by his son, R. H. Gardiner 2nd, whose addenda have now been printed as footnotes. Recently the text has been carefully compared with the original manuscript at Oaklands, by the author's great-granddaughter Alice Gardiner, and great-great-grandson Tudor Gardiner. The undersigned great-grandson, R. H. Gardiner 4th, assumes responsibility for having used scissors and paste to rearrange the order of the text under chapter headings, but further changes seemed undesirable.

Robert Hallowell Gardiner
William Tudor Gardiner

Oaklands, 1936.

CONTENTS

ILLUSTRATIONS

HALLOWELL

BENJAMIN HALLOWELL
1699-1773
m.
Rebecca Briggs
1699-1795

- REBECCA HALLOWELL 1723-
  m. Captain Thomas Bishop, R. N.
- BENJAMIN HALLOWELL 1725-1799
  m. Mary Boylston 1722.
  - WARD HALLOWELL
    later Ward Nicholas Boylston
    1749-1827
  - Admiral Sir BENJAMIN HALLOWELL, R.N., K. C. B., later Benjamin Hallowell Carew
    1761-1834
  - MARY HALLOWELL
    1762-
    m. John A. Elmsley, Chief Justice of Canada
- SARAH HALLLOWELL 1727-1809
  m. Samuel Vaughan 1720-1802
  - For their children see page 118
- BRIGGS HALLOWELL 1728-1778
  m. Eunice......
- MARY HALLOWELL 1732-1762
  unmarried
- ANNE HALLOWELL 1735-1812
  m. Lt.-Col. Sir C. C. Gould, Bart.
  - their daughter Mrs. Gee devised the Carew properties to Admiral Hallowell
- SAMUEL HALLOWELL 1737-
  unmarried
- ROBERT HALLOWELL 1739-1818
  m. Hannah Gardiner 1744-1796
  - Four daughters, all of whom died unmarried, and one son, ROBERT HALLOWELL 1782-1864, writer of these memoirs, who added the name of Gardiner in 1803.

CHAPTER 1

THE HALLOWELL FAMILY

Oaklands, 1861

I have been so frequently and so strongly urged by the different members of my family to make for them a sketch of my early life and early residence in Maine that for their satisfaction I will endeavor to recall some of the events of that distant period.

My father's family originated, I believe, in Devonshire and according to Savage emigrated first to Connecticut, but from deeds which I had once in my possession were settled in Boston before the close of the 17th century.

My grandfather, Benjamin Hallowell, was extensively engaged in shipbuilding, in the fishing on the banks of Newfoundland, and in foreign commerce. He was one of the large proprietors in the Kennebec Purchase and owned a valuable and extensive estate in Boston, embracing several acres with a large water front, and extending from Liberty Square to Fort Hill.

This estate he divided by will between my uncle Benjamin and my father, and by purchase from his brother my father became possessed of the whole. My grandfather, in an age of narrowness and bigotry, was distinguished for his liberality of sentiment and public spirit. The poet Greene, in a satirical poem upon a Masonic procession, applied to him the characteristic of 'Nobleness of Soul.' My grandfather was a member of the Old South Church in Boston when the clergy had not relinquished their control over the laity, and the pastor of that society, Dr. Sewall, when he perceived that my grandfather was absent from meeting, invariably called the next day to ascertain the cause of his staying away.

My grandfather would not submit to this strict discipline, but, being Navy agent, thought it proper to contribute to the erection of King's Chapel, and occasionally accompanied some of the British officers to worship there. His duties as Navy agent brought him into frequent intercourse with the naval officers and his cordial hospitality made his home a pleasant resort for those of both services. He died in January 1773, at the age of 74 years.

His widow, who had been prostrated by a stroke of paralysis and for two weeks lay wholly unconscious, life being sustained by oysters taken without exertion on her part, recovered her faculties and accompanied my uncle Benjamin to England, where she survived for 20 years, dying in London at the advanced age of 96. Her children employed her niece Patty Hallowell to take care of her and settled upon her an annuity for life.

Their oldest son, Benjamin, tho' not an officer in the navy, commanded several vessels of war, in 1746 a privateer and subsequently two King's ships, the 'King George' and the 'Robert.' His original commissions are preserved by the Antiquarian Society in Worcester, who have also his commission as Justice of the Peace with a stamped certificate attached that he had partaken of the communion at the church of St. Martin's in the Fields. He was Collector of the Customs at Boston, then Comptroller, and subsequently one of the Commissioners of the Customs for all the colonies, and a Mandamus Counsellor. These two last offices were both extremely obnoxious to the patriots. The Commissioners were clothed with arbitrary powers and were appointed in order to stop the very profitable but illegal traffic carried on between the New England colonies and the West Indies, and the Mandamus Counsellors had authority which interfered with the privileges of Massachusetts under its charter. The exercise of these powers made him extremely unpopular. His house in Hanover Street was attacked by a mob who completely sacked it. He was driven out of it with his family and took refuge in the country. After the evacuation of Boston he went to England, but returned in 1796 and died in Canada.

My father [Robert Hallowell] was the second *[fourth]

*Editor's Note. The vital records of Boston, followed in the table on page 2, disagree with the author as to the order of birth of his father's generation.

son and received a mercantile education and tho' not engaged in any regular business of his own, he assisted his father in his extensive concerns and was employed by him in superintending the erection of a saw mill at Abadagasset about the year 1766. He was subsequently appointed Collector of Portsmouth, then the second town in importance in New England. He was at this time engaged to my mother and of course passed frequently between that place and Boston. He was on intimate terms with many of the British officers on the station, and as they had little real duty, they would frequently propose to save him a tedious journey and take him in their frigate to his post in New Hampshire.

The morals of Portsmouth at that time were below those of the country generally, particularly among those who claimed to form the first class in society. Indeed, from the various anecdotes told me by my father of what occurred within his own knowledge, I have no doubt that vice was quite as prevalent in New England, though not so conspicuous, a century ago as at any time since, notwithstanding the sanctity of manners claimed by the Puritan fathers and the rigid and scrutinizing discipline enforced by them.

It was customary in Boston, and probably throughout New England, to have family prayers at 9 o'clock in the evening, when all retired to their chambers. The young men remained there till about 10, when they supposed the old folks to be quietly asleep; they then went out to their clubs and parties. As the young people went to these parties without the knowledge, and against the wills of their parents, they indulged in greater license, and scenes have been related to me that would shock the most liberal of the present day. I shall have occasion again to speak of my father.

The 3rd son, Samuel, died a bachelor before his father, but I know nothing of his history.

The youngest [second], to whom his mother's maiden name of Briggs was given, resided at Hallowell on a tract of 3000 acres given him by my grandfather. He seems to have been inefficient and died poor. He had mortgaged the land to my grandfather Gardiner, and Mr. Samuel Vaughan, who had married his sister, bought the right of redemption from Briggs' widow and came into possession of this property, on which some of the children still reside.

Mr. Samuel Vaughan was a London merchant but came to Boston occasionally to procure supplies for his Jamaica plantation, and there became acquainted with my grandfather's oldest [second] daughter, whom he married. He was concerned with my grandfather in some mercantile speculations which proved unsuccessful.

My grandfather's second [fourth] daughter married Lt. Col. C. C. Gould, one of the oldest baronets in England. His nephew has been recently advanced to the peerage, by the title of Lord Tredegar.

The third daughter, Mary, lost her life in the great fire in 1762, which destroyed her father's mansion house and a large number of stores and other buildings belonging to him and on which there was no insurance, there being no insurance offices in the country at this time.

The youngest [oldest] daughter, Rebecca, married Capt. Bishop, of the British Navy, who commanded the sloop of war 'Lively' at the battle of Bunker Hill.

My uncle Benjamin left two sons and a daughter.

The second son, Benjamin, entered the British Navy before the commencement of the Revolutionary War and became a distinguished officer, and various orders were conferred upon him for gallant conduct. In the Battle of the Nile he commanded the Swiftsure of 74 guns under Lord Nelson. After the victory all the officers presented to the admiral some memorial from the wreck. Capt. Hallowell fixed upon a most remarkable present, a coffin made from the mainmast of the French admiral's ship, 'L'Orient', of 120 guns, which he had assisted to blow up. This present Nelson highly valued, kept it in his cabin, and directed that he should be conveyed in it to his last resting place.

The oldest son, named Ward, went to England. Before establishing himself in business, he travelled extensively, and, what was unusual in those days, visited Palestine and Egypt. A mummy which he brought from there was the first ever seen in the United States. He subsequently established himself in London as a merchant, and being intimate in Lord Chesterfield's family, was made one of his executors. Upon becoming the heir of his maternal uncle Nicholas Boylston, he changed his name from Hallowell to Boylston.

The uncle [Nicholas Boylston] was a character almost as remarkable for his miserly disposition as the famous Elwees. He had always lived a bachelor and from his shrewdness in business and his parsimonious habits had acquired a very large fortune. At the breaking out of the revolution he took what he believed to be the strongest side and became a refugee. To save his extensive real estate from confiscation, he conveyed it to his brother-in-law Moses Gill, afterwards Lt. Governor and acting Governor of Massachusetts, but carried with him a very large sum for those days; I believe nearly £100,000.

In London he applied to Mr. Manning for advice as to the best mode of investment and when he was told the public funds, he replied that they did not give sufficient interest. Mr. M. then observed to him that he was an old man past 70, without anyone dependent upon him, and, as with his habits he would not spent a tithe of the income that the funds would give him, why should he trouble himself about a larger income. 'Sir', he replied, 'if I had a pile of gold that reached from earth to heaven, and I could by any exertion add a guinea to the heap, I should be unhappy till I had accomplished it'. In striving to add the additional guinea he overset the whole and became a bankrupt. The house of Lane, Son, & Frazier tempted him to loan them his money, giving a bond to employ it in the contraband trade with South America, with a guarantee that it should yield 12 per cent profit. Upon their failure, the creditors told him that he was either a partner with that firm, or had lent them money at usurious interest, and he might take either horn of the dilemma that he chose. He would do neither but went to jail. In jail his love of thrift did not forsake him, and he would have retailed coals to the other prisoners in order, as he expressed it, to make a penny, if the jailer would have allowed it, and when ill in jail my uncle, who was then in narrow circumstances himself, was obliged to furnish him with such medical advice and comforts as his situation required. After remaining in jail a year, he compromised with the creditors of Lane, Son, & Frazier, taking all their property and paying 50 per cent of their debts.

Ward Nicholas Boylston, his nephew and heir, returned to Boston in order to recover the property placed in the hands of Moses Gill. This he accomplished after tedious law suits, and compromised with the town of Boston for a legacy bequeathed to them by his uncle, which was by its terms to accumulate at compound interest till it should amount to a sum sufficient to purchase the land in Boston between State St. and the Market and extending from Exchange St. to Merchants Row, and to erect upon it a splendid exchange—a devise incapable of execution, as the land with the expensive buildings constantly put upon it was increasing in value more rapidly than the money at interest.

Ward Nicholas Boylston, tho' not a physician, took a strong interest in the promotion of medical science, his maternal grandfather having been very distinguished in the profession and being the first to introduce into America inoculation for the smallpox.

Ward Boylston gave a very valuable medical library to Harvard University, and left a fund sufficient to keep it always supplied with new medical works, and another fund for prizes for the best medical disputations. His uncle had left a legacy to the college for the support of a professor of oratory, which had become forfeited. This he restored, reserving to himself the appointment of the first professor. The person he named was his relative, John Quincy Adams, afterward President of the United States. He meant to have bequeathed the bulk of his fortune to the college, but he did not think they conferred upon him the distinctions to which he considered his donations entitled him. Dr. Kirkland, the president, had a great dislike to Boylston, and I had several conversations with the doctor upon the subject. I expressed my opinion that if the college chose to accept his gifts they were bound to comply with his expectations in conferring them. Boylston had much of his uncle's love of money and of his unwillingness to part with it, of which a remarkable instance occurs to me. He was indebted to his brother, the admiral, who had in vain tried by letter to obtain a settlement. He then sent a full power to Mr. Benjamin Vaughan to settle in any way that he could. Mr. V. did not like to undertake it and wished me to do it, to which I assented. Finding Boylston unwilling to make any arrangement, and understanding his character, I observed to him that if it was inconvenient to him to pay the money, his brother would be satisfied with a post obit bond. He jumped at this at once, told me to examine the papers carefully and he would sign the bond for the amount I found due, which he did; yet I had reason to suppose that he had then deposited in bank enough to pay the debt and for which he had no particular use, and he knew his brother had a large family with small means to support them.

Another instance will show the bent of his mind. Dining with him once, he opened a bottle of very old wine and observed to the company, 'This wine, adding compound interest to its cost, is worth a crown a glass.' To which Commodore Bainbridge, who was one of the company, replied, 'I hate compound interest, let us circulate the bottle and get rid of it as quickly as possible.'

My uncle's only daughter, Mary, married John Elmsley, who in the autumn of 1796 received the appointment of Chief Justice of Upper, and subsequently, of Lower Canada, and as it was necessary for him at once to take possession of his office, he came with his wife and her father to Boston on his way thither. Western New York was then a wilderness where travellers passing thru' were obliged to encamp for one or two nights. Judge Elmsley, thinking neither his wife or my uncle could bear the exposure at the advanced season, left them at my father's till the milder weather of the following spring. My uncle, from his former unpopularity, felt some uneasiness as to the reception he would meet upon his return to the place of his nativity, but all grievances seemed to have been forgotten, and he was welcomed with very great cordiality and was in a round of parties during the whole winter. Mrs. Elmsley had a fine understanding, a warm heart, and was very agreeable in her manner and conversation, and during her five months residence in the family endeared herself very much to them.

After my uncle removed to Canada he received the grant of a township of land, and died in the province in the year 1798, at the age of 76.

Their descendants still reside in Canada.

GARDINER

Parent	Children	Descendants
DR. SILVESTER GARDINER 1707-1786 m. Anne Gibbons	COUNSELLOR JOHN GARDINER 1731-1793 m. Margaret Harries of Wales	Several children including Rev. John Silvester John Gardiner 1765-1830
	WILLIAM GARDINER -1787 d. unmarried	
	ANNE GARDINER -1807 m. Col. Arthur Browne, son of Earl of Altamont	their descendants now living in Ireland and England
	HANNAH GARDINER 1744-1796 m. Robert Hallowell	four daughters, all of whom died unmarried, and one son Robert Hallowell, writer of these memoirs, who took the name of Robert Hallowell Gardiner, 1782-1864
	REBECCA GARDINER m. Philip Dumaresq	several children, of whom a son James and a daughter Mrs. Thomas Handasyde Perkins lived on Swan Island
	ABIGAIL GARDINER m. Oliver Whipple	Silvester Gardiner Whipple, unmarried Hannah m. Frederic Allen

CHAPTER 2

THE GARDINER FAMILY

My mother was the daughter of Dr. Silvester* Gardiner, who was fourth in descent from William Gardiner, one of the first emigrants from England to Rhode Island. He settled on the south side of Narragansett Bay, and a portion of his lands still remain in the possession of his posterity.

Dr. Silvester Gardiner was born in Narragansett in 1707. His father, William, was a lawyer and, as was not unusual in those primitive days, united the cultivation of a farm with the practice of his profession. Though not wealthy, he had a competent estate and gave his children the best education the country afforded. His second daughter was married to the Rev. Dr. McSparran, a gentleman of learning and ability who laboured in Narragansett as a missionary of the Society for the Propagation of the Gospel for a period of thirty-seven years. He had a great influence on the future life of his brother-in-law Silvester, whose education he undertook to direct. He first sent him to school in Boston, which at that early day had acquired a reputation for the excellence of its schools. He subsequently directed his studies himself, and approved of his selection of the practice of medicine as his future profession. Endowed with uncommon vigour of intellect, Silvester sought in vain in his own country for the aid which was indispensably necessary to the proper knowledge of his profession. There were neither hospitals nor medical schools in the country, and the medical practitioner, with scarcely any knowledge of the wonderful structure of the human frame and the functions of its numerous and complicated organs, was obliged to grope his way in the dark, with only the limited experience which he and those around him had acquired in this

*Sometimes spelt Sylvester.

DR. SILVESTER GARDINER

By Copley

practice. The religious prejudices of the community were inimical to the study of anatomy, and fully sustained the severe enactments which existed against the procuring of subjects for dissection. The ashes of the dead were not to be disturbed, even when there were no friends whose feelings might thereby be wounded, though information was to be gained which might preserve the lives of the living. Silvester knew that these prejudices did not exist in Europe, that medicine had there become a science, and that in Paris there was every facility for the study of anatomy without a knowledge of which the healing art was mere empiricism. He, therefore, felt an ardent desire to obtain this knowledge which his own country did not afford. His father was in comfortable circumstances, but had a large family to support, and his expenses while pursuing his studies in Europe would make a large draught upon the paternal property. He therefore proposed to his father to advance to him enough for his education in Europe, in lieu of all expectation from the family estate. This request was readily granted, and he went immediately to Europe where he spent eight years pursuing his studies with great assiduity in London and Edinburgh and Paris, particularly in the latter city, and thus acquired knowledge, skill and reputation which secured for him future wealth and distinction. His sojourn in Paris was during the Orleans regency, the most dissolute and disgraceful period in French history. The open profligacy of the French at that period gave him great dislike to their character which continued into after life, and he would not permit his children to learn French lest they should be tempted to read licentious and irreligious literature which the French press was continually pouring forth for the gratification and amusement of the Court.

Upon Dr. Gardiner's return from Europe, he settled in Boston as a physician, where he very soon obtained very extensive and lucrative practice. He brought with him a valuable collection of anatomical specimens and gave a course of lectures upon anatomy. Soon after his settlement in Boston he became acquainted with and engaged the affections of Anne Gibbons, daughter of a wealthy physician, Dr. William Gibbons, whom he married. It being difficult at that time to procure pure and unadulterated medicine, Dr. Gardiner determined to establish a druggist store and he became a very large importer, supplying almost all the apothecaries in New England with their drugs and medicines.* His business and extensive practice gave him great affluence and enabled him to indulge his hospitable disposition and his taste for society. All distinguished visitors were constantly guests at his house, and among them were many officers of the army and navy of Great Britain, some of whom were highly connected. This cultivated society fostered the attachment to the mother country which he had imbibed when in Europe, and had an important influence on his future life. Though he lived in this hospitable style and entertained a great deal of the best company and kept his carriage, he yet lived with a certain degree of simplicity.

His druggist store was on Washington Street and his estate extended back to Winter Street, upon which now stands the Music Hall. His dwelling house was back of his druggist store, and thro' it was the entrance to his house. His children as they grew up felt unwilling that their guests should be carried thro' the shop and wished their father to make an entrance to the house from Winter Street, but this he would not do, telling them that he would never be ashamed of any business in which he was engaged and that so long as he kept a druggist store, so long should be the entrance thro' it to his house. Col. Browne, the second son of the Earl of Altamont, made his visits in this way to the

*Note of R. H. G. 2nd.

Dr. Gardiner's drug store was at the corner of Washington and Winter Streets, his lot extending half way to Tremont Street, his residence being upon Winter Street. While living there he was much annoyed by a favorite negro slave, by name Hasard. He one day, having taken offence at his master, put poison into the coffee prepared for breakfast, but being attached to Mrs. Gardiner, cautioned her against tasting it. The doctor overlooked this, but subsequently Hasard set fire to his master's stable. The neighbors then remonstrated, saying that the doctor might submit to be poisoned if he chose, but when it came to incendiarism, it was more than they would endure. Dr. Gardiner yielded to these remonstrances, and sent Hasard to Kennebec, giving him a farm upon the Cobbossee at a place which still bears his name. Subsequently a very protracted lawsuit ensued between two towns as to the support of Hasard or his descendants, the question turning upon the point whether Hasard, being a slave, had gained a legal residence. Tom Lewis, who lived on the river bank below Nahumkeag, was his grandson.

MRS. SILVESTER GARDINER

By Copley

house while he was paying his addresses to my aunt whom he afterward married.

He never engaged in politics. In early life his profession and the business of a druggist fully occupied his time, though he took an active part in church affairs and was engaged in the rebuilding of King's Chapel of which he was many years warden, and in which he owned two pews which were taken by the church when it became Unitarian.

Dr. Silvester Gardiner left two sons and four daughters.

The oldest son, John, was sent at an early age to Great Britain for his education, and after studying in Scotland and travelling in England, became a student at law in the Inner Temple. Upon being admitted to the bar, he commenced practice in the Welsh circuit. He then married a Miss Harris, a near connection of Sir Watkins Wm. Wynn, distinguished in English political life. She was a posthumous child for whom no provision was made in her father's will. She would not allow the will to be set aside, because if it had been, an estate bequeathed to her younger brother would have passed with the other real estate to the oldest, and the youngest would have been left without any provision. This brother wished to give this estate to his sister Gardiner, but died a few days before he attained the age to make the bequest legal, and the estate came into the possession of the elder brother, who retained it.

My uncle John was a most extraordinary character. His talents were of a high order, and he had a most uncommon memory and was a fine classical scholar. Your uncle William Tudor spent a summer with him, and as they rode together on horseback, he would repeat long passages from his favorite Latin and Greek authors, particularly from Homer. He was a man of strong feelings, ardent temperament, violent temper, and great eccentricity. After practising for a time in the Welsh circuit, he removed to the great sphere of London and soon gained the notice and favor of Lord Mansfield, and with his patronage and his own ability the highest honors of the profession seemed within his reach. But he adopted ultra Whig principles, associated with Wilkes, Churchill, and persons of that character, and when Wilkes was arrested and tried on a general Secretary of State's warrant, Gardiner was junior counsel in the defence. The trial was considered of great importance as testing a great political principle. This was not formally decided, as Wilkes was acquitted upon a technical point, but the illegality of the warrant was so clearly proved that no attempt has since been made to issue it. Gardiner had a handsome piece of plate presented to him after the occasion, now in the possession of his grandson, Wm. H. Gardiner of Boston. There is a long inscription on it complimenting him on his successful exertions in proving the illegality of a general Secretary of State's warrent, *'This canker of English liberty.'* He of course lost the favour of Lord Mansfield, who however retained sufficient interest in him to obtain for him the appointment of Attorney General of St. Kitts as an honorable banishment. He did not then conceal his republican sentiments and by the active part he took in opposition to the Government made himself so obnoxious to the authorities that he deemed it expedient privately to leave the island, and after a short residence in Jamaica established himself in Martinique, where he obtained an extensive practice and took office under the French Government.

At the close of the war, he returned to this country. In a letter to his father, dated Boston, July 14, 1783, he says, 'Gov. Hancock, Saml. Adams, D. Cooper, &c. have all received me with the greatest cordiality, and Genl. Washington, in consequence of a letter from the French Ministry, overwhelmed me with civility during the four days I staid with him.' He opened an office in Boston, and, notwithstanding his republican notions, he persuaded the bar to resume the legal costume which had been laid aside. Not liking to walk thro' the street in their gowns, they robed at your grandfather Tudor's, whose house was next to the Court House. The custom was not of long continuance and was said to have been given up on account of a countryman hearing Hitchborne use very profane language while chaffering for a load of wood, and expressing his astonishment that a Boston minister should swear so, the black gown having made him suppose that Hitchborne was a clergyman.

In his religious opinions my uncle was an Arian and took

an active part in altering the liturgy of the King's Chapel, which his father had liberally contributed to build, and of which he had been for many years a warden. The alteration at the time was simply to omit or change what related to the Trinity. He gave my mother a copy of the altered liturgy and signed his name to the preface to show that he was its author. A majority of the pewholders, being royalists, abandoned the country. Those who remained employed Mr. James Freeman as a lay reader, who was refused episcopal ordination when he applied for it on account of his Arian sentiments. His wardens then undertook to ordain him by the imposition of hands. As one was a tobacconist and the other a physician, it gave rise to the witticism that he had been ordained by snuff and diachylon.

When in Boston he [John Gardiner] would go to Trinity Church, where his son was assistant minister, saying that he must hear Jack preach, and while the congregation were making the responses from the Book of Common Prayer, he would make them in an audible voice from the chapel liturgy. Upon the death of his wife in 1786 he removed with his children to the property bequeathed to them in Pownalboro'.

Many anecdotes are related of his eccentricity and of the petty frauds practised upon him by his unlearned but cunning neighbors. As soon as he was established at Pownalboro', he was elected to the General Court, where his determined and unyielding character was at once shown.

Before taking his seat, he was required to be naturalized upon the ground that having been out of the country during the whole revolutionary war, he had thereby lost his citizenship. To this he replied that he had been sent at an early age to England for his education, long before the trouble of the revolution commenced, that he had always been a republican, and as he had never done anything to forfeit his citizenship, he demanded his seat in the House as a citizen of the Commonwealth of Massachusetts. The House, unable to make him yield, to save their dignity passed a resolve which was highly complimentary to him, declaring him and his three children by name to be American citizens, thus in reality yielding the point in dispute and allowing him at once to take his seat.

When in the Legislature he perceived that many of the laws in the English code, which were binding upon us, were not adapted to a new and democratic country like ours, and he set himself actively and energetically at work to reform them. He was successful in procuring the passage of a law abolishing primogeniture and another virtually abolishing entails. He was not equally successful in doing away with special pleading, where he was before his age. They feared him as too great an innovator, but in recent times special pleading has been wholly abolished or greatly modified in most of our states, and even in England. He aided in obtaining a repeal of the law against theatrical entertainment. He had prepared a very learned speech upon the occasion, full of Latin and Greek quotations which he was told would be wholly above the comprehension of his audience, and he acceded to the advice of printing it instead of delivering it in the House of Representatives. It makes a respectable octavo volume.

My grandfather, to show his disapprobation of my uncle's opinions, both in religion and politics, which he considered dangerous to the welfare of the community, left him by will only a guinea, bequeathing his proportion of his estate to my uncle's children, but by a codicil, bearing even date with the will, he left him £1000 sterling, and to his eldest son, the half of Swan Island, five miles in length; and by another codicil, dated a few days subsequently, he bequeathed to the same grandson, J. S. J. Gardiner, a very valuable estate in Washington St., Boston, which he had received from his father-in-law, Gibbons. This had been confiscated, sold, and bought in by the State, but by the treaties of 1783 was restored to its rightful owner. By another codicil, he gave one-half the Pownalboro' estate and mills to my uncle and the other half to his children.

Tho' I could have been only between 11 and 12 when he died, I have a distinct recollection of his appearance—his short stout person, his hair tied up in a silk bag, and his quick, loud, and commanding voice. I recollect his coming into our house one day and after sitting in the parlour for a moment, complaining of the excessive heat and making my mother go down into the cellar to talk with him, as being the only cool place he could find.

In the winter he slept in a chest as it was much warmer than sleeping on a bedstead. A hole was cut in the lid of the chest to allow him to breathe. He retired early and it was said that his guests would sometimes after he had retired play cards on the chest and that he would occasionally cry out that he could not sleep if they struck the chest so hard with their knuckles.

In the autumn of 1793, my uncle embarked from Pownalboro in a schooner with a very heavy deck load bound for Boston; the wind was blowing violently from the north west, and almost immediately on leaving the river the vessel was overset by a sudden gust of wind, and my uncle, with all on board, perished. He was then in the 63rd year of his age.

Of the second son, William, I shall have occasion to speak hereafter.

The eldest daughter, Anne, married Col. Browne, an Irish officer in the British service. He was the second son of the Earl of Altamont, and his older brother being very sickly in his youth, my aunt expected to be able to place a coronet on her coach, but in this she was disappointed. Her brother-in-law recovered his health and lived to vote for the union of Ireland with England, for which service he was made Marquis of Sligo.

My mother Hannah was the second daughter.

The third married Philip Dumaresq. Her father was displeased with the match, principally, I believe, because Dumaresq was without property and was in no business by which he could support a family, and, to show his displeasure, he left the property designed for his daughter in trust for her use during her life and then to go to her daughters, to the exclusion of the sons, to whom he left only a legacy of 1600 acres of land in Pittston. Dumaresq was said to have had pleasing gentlemanly manners, looking for support to the patronage of persons in authority rather than to his own exertions. He was at one time aide de camp to Lord Dunmore, Governor of New Jersey, and through his influence obtained some little office in Abaca, one of the Bahamas, where he lived in great poverty. He subsequently obtained the Collectorship of Nassau, New Providence. He left three sons and two daughters, of whom I shall have occasion to speak hereafter.

My grandfather's youngest daughter, Abigail, remained single till all the other children had left the paternal roof, till her mother had deceased, and till my grandfather had married again. His second wife was a Mrs. Eppes, a widow, daughter of Mr. Pickman of Salem, and much younger than himself. Previous to my grandfather's second marriage, the children were on the same familiar terms with him as before they had establishments of their own, and he was very glad to have them come to him whenever they chose without invitation, but as soon as the second Mrs. Gardiner was established in the family, she gave them to understand that invitations would be sent to them whenever their company was desired and she made Abigail's situation at home very uncomfortable.

Abigail differed entirely from the rest of the family. She was quite plain, had not much sense and not a pleasant temper, and was not pleasing in her manners. She found her situation at home with her step-mother so uncomfortable that she was glad to accept the offered hand of Oliver Whipple.

Whipple was of a good family in Providence, a graduate of Harvard and not deficient in natural ability, but he was without any fixed principle, floating on the surface of society and yielding to the current, careless whither it might carry him. He commenced the practice of law at Portsmouth, N. H., but having little business, lived on his wife's property, which he greatly mismanaged. As the marriage had been originally contracted without affection on either side, indifference soon grew into dislike, which gendered anger and quarrelling, till the union became too insufferable to be longer borne, and each party sued for a divorce.

Whipple was always an inmate at my father's when he

came to Boston, and my father aided him to pay many of his son Silvester's college bills, which he was unable to do himself; yet Mrs. Whipple took an aversion to the family because I was preferred to her son by my grandfather in his will, and none of the family were allowed to enter her doors. My father no sooner heard of their divorce suits, and that Whipple was endeavoring to find evidence to blacken his wife's character, for which I believe there was no ground, than he hurried down to their residence at Hampton to prevent, if possible, the prosecution of his suit, tho' he was himself in the greatest affliction, his eldest daughter, the object of his tenderest affection, having just deceased and lying unburied. By representing to Whipple the very injurious effect it would have upon their children, he induced him to withdraw his suit and allow the divorce to be granted on her complaint against him. After the separation Mrs. Whipple took her son to manage her affairs, but he had no more knowledge of business than a child, and the property was melting away faster than before. The parents recollected that there were advantages in their union, he to have something to live upon, and she to have some one to take care of what she had left. They therefore agreed to forget their former bickerings, and were married again and removed to Hallowell.

I felt unwilling to live in the vicinity of such near connexions and entirely estranged from them, particularly as they had become poor. Your mother and I called upon them, and I then saw her for the first time in my life. As their means became nearly exhausted, Whipple went to Washington, where he obtained a clerkship which he retained till his death, and Mrs. Whipple removed to her daughter Allen's in this place, where she remained till she died. We were on friendly terms with her children, and had Mrs. Whipple occasionally to dine with us.

My uncle [John Gardiner] left two sons and a daughter. The oldest, John Sylvester John, commenced the study of law in your grandfather Tudor's office, but his mind was not logical, and the other young men in the office not being industrious, he took a dislike to the profession, and commenced the study of divinity. While pursuing his studies with his father in Pownalboro' he read prayers during one summer where Jacob Bailey, the Border Missionary, had laboured for so many years. Upon being ordained, he accepted an invitation to the Episcopal church at Beaufort, S. C. After remaining a year, he became assistant minister at Trinity Church, Boston, and upon the death of Bishop Parker, succeeded him as rector. He married the daughter of Col. Howard of Augusta, and his family and ours became very intimate. Supper was then the social meal, and we partook of it together at one or the other house as often as once or twice a week. For economy they removed to Brookline, and always made my father's house their stopping place in Boston for themselves and their horse.

There grew up a warm friendship between the Dr. and myself, tho' he was 16 years my senior, nor was it in the least interrupted when I became old enough to have formed decided opinions upon important subjects, which I freely expressed, tho' they differed from his own.

This friendship descended to our children. When the Dr. went for his health with his wife and daughter Louisa to England, their other daughter Elizabeth came to live with us and remained in our family about 15 months till the return of her mother after the death of her father. Elizabeth had a very fine understanding, which her father had taken great pains to cultivate. She went thro' the same course of studies as the boys in his school. She had a warm heart, great brilliancy in conversation, and deep views of religion. She and your sister Emma became very dear friends. After Louisa's marriage to Mr. Cushing, she and her mother resided in Temple Place in a house which Mr. Cushing purchased for them, and there I went and always found a home and a most cordial welcome whenever I was in Boston. We have been less intimate with her brother William, tho' I have reason to believe the hereditary friendship is still retained by him.

January 7th, 1772, my father married Hannah, second daughter of Dr. Silvester Gardiner. The wedding had been postponed some weeks on account of the illness of his father. Soon after his marriage, his brother, upon being made Commissioner of Customs, relinquished his office of Collector of the Port of Boston in favour of my father, who received the appointment.

CHAPTER 3

REFUGEES

In November 1773, the famous destruction of tea took place in Boston harbour, in consequence of which the British Parliament passed an Act shutting up the port after the succeeding 17th of June and ordering the custom house to be removed to Salem, but the Salem people at a public meeting voted that they wished not to profit by the misfortunes of their neighbors in having the custom house transferred from Boston to their town, and the Commissioners ordered my father to remove his office to Plymouth. He did not remove his family, but, having little business to do, only remained there two or three days in the week.

The troubles increasing, the British undertook to retain Boston by their army, but Genl. Washington, by his skilful movements in cutting off all supplies for the army, obliged the evacuation of the town in March, 1776. The principal loyalists left with the troops, abandoning their country, many never to see it again. Some went to New York, where the Crown retained its power for a longer period. Some to England by the way of Nova Scotia, among whom was my father and his family. My father remained at Halifax for some months, and there my sister Anne was born. Others made that province their permanent residence, and several of their descendants have become distinguished.

My father, upon first going to England, resided in London, but subsequently in Bristol, to which place many of his American friends were attracted by the reputed cheapness of living, it having been for many years declining both in business and population, and there I was born, February 10th, 1782. His sisters Gould and Bishop, upon becoming widows, made Bristol their place of residence. The royalists in abandoning their country were obliged also to abandon their property, which was confiscated by the state governments for public use. Little, however, found its way into the treasury, for as the law directed that creditors of the loyalists should be paid out of the proceeds of the sales of their property, claims were brought whose validity there was no one to dispute and which absorbed the greater portion of the sales. I was once walking with my father after his return to this country, when he met a person who had presented, and been allowed, a claim upon his estate. He asked the man how he could present such a claim when he knew that he did not owe him anything. The man replied, 'I would not, Mr. Hallowell, wrong you for the world. The account I presented to the commissioners was correct. I only omitted to say that you had paid it. I knew the presentation could do you no harm. Everybody was doing the same, and I was much in want of money.' Most of the American loyalists, having left their property behind, found themselves after their arrival in England, in straitened circumstances. They had applied to Government for relief, but little was granted till after the year of 1783, when their claims were allowed, and my father received a pension of £220 sterling per annum.

My father, from the grace and amenity of his manners, soon made friends who procured for him various small agencies which enabled him with strict economy to support his family and educate his children. The celebrated Hannah More and her sister kept at that time a school for young ladies at Bristol and my two sisters, both older than myself, were placed under their tuition.

Boys at that time in England were kept in petticoats until they were 6 or 7 years of age, and I recollect the first time I was dressed in a long coat and breeches (the costume then of boys), standing on a chair in the window all the morning to show myself to those passing. So early is the love of distinction developed. As soon as I was old enough I was sent to an excellent school at Stapleton a few miles from Bristol, of which the Rev. Mr. Cockagne, perpetual curate of the parish, was the master. In commencing Latin no translations were allowed, and the grammar was in that language without a syllable of English to facilitate the remembrance of the genders of Latin nouns, which are altogether arbitrary. The nouns were put into doggerel verse with the proper article prefixed, and this committed to memory, and tho' it is now more than 70 years since I was thus exercised, the jingle of the rhymes still occasionally occurs to my memory. The discipline of the school was strict but not harsh. The missing of a single word was invariably followed by the delinquent being mounted on the back of another boy, and the birch applied to his bare flesh, which was preceded by a short lecture, and followed by a bread and cheese dinner. The birch was not applied so as to inflict pain, but the disgrace was considered so great that these punishments were not of frequent occurrence. The principal reward was being invited to take tea with the master in his study, and, in the season, he very freely distributed among the boys fruit from an excellent garden, which in consequence never suffered any depredations. There was a peculiar custom in the school, that every new comer should try his strength by fighting other boys of his own size, but the older boys never allowed the stronger to tyrannize over the weaker, and I was never at a school where there was less quarrelling.

In 1786 my grandfather Gardiner died at Newport, R. I. at the age of 79. He had left this country reluctantly, from the importunity of his young wife, who was very desirous to visit England. Dr. Lloyd and several of his friends who held tory sentiments like himself remained in the country, and by keeping perfectly quiet and not talking upon politics, they suffered very little annoyance. He returned as soon after the war as practicable.

By his will, as my father was out of the country, Oliver Whipple was joined with him as executor, but he evidenced his intention that the settlement of the estate should devolve principally upon my father by allowing him an annuity for doing the business.

My grandfather designed this estate [Gardiner, Maine] for my uncle William. In the year 1759 he sent him to England to purchase goods to enable him to open a store in this place, and beside paying the expenses of the journey gave him a bill of exchange for £1000 sterling on London. Upon his return he came down here to take charge of this property upon which my grandfather had built mills, and of which William seems to have been allowed to receive the income.* With a handsome person and mild gentlemanly manners, but with no force of mind and no energy and great self-indulgence, he was poorly qualified to cope with the pioneers of the wilderness, who despised him for his gentleness and hated him for his tory connections. He was kept in a constant state of terror, and he yielded to their threats what he would not to their persuasions. He was at one time arrested as inimical to the revolutionary government, but according to his own account, the real cause was his attempting to restrain those who were plundering his property. The evidence produced was that he had spoken harshly of three of the justices before whom he was tried, and who packed a jury to convict him. They sent him to the military committee in Boston. But the trial was so irregular that the judgment was set aside and he was released. My grandfather seemed to have reposed but little confidence in his son's judgment. He gave him a power only to lease and no power to sell any portion of this property. When the process of confiscation was commenced, William, knowing that his father meant eventually to give him this property, thought that he might claim it as his own to save it, and for this purpose forged a deed of the estate from his father to himself, which he kept to be produced when necessary and which he neglected to destroy when no longer wanted.

The first attempt at confiscation in Maine was made so irregularly that it was found necessary to commence the proofs anew, and before the second attempt was consummated, the Peace of 1783 put a stop to all governmental alienation of private property. Soon after the peace, my

*Note of R. H. G. 2nd.

Mr. William Gardiner's residence was near the house built by Nathan Bridge, now occupied by Bernard Esmond. It was a large and handsome house, the plans of which were still not long since in a portfolio at Oaklands, but I think it was never completed, and that Mr. Gardiner died in a small house in which he had always lived nearby. The grounds as laid out were to extend with a gradual slope to the river.

grandfather sent Mr. Whipple down to ascertain the situation of the property and to report upon his son's management. Whipple took William with him and calling upon the various persons in occupancy of any portion of the property made them take leases from them jointly, a clear evidence that William never had the intention to claim the property against his father by virtue of the forged deed. William could not have realized much income during the war, but in 1784 he leased the mills for £2000 lawful, $6666.66 per annum.

In the year 1787 William died from taking an overdose of laudanum to allay the pain of a violent colic, and, as he died childless, this property, by my grandfather's will, devolved upon me. My father was also executor to his own father, whose estate, owing to the revolutionary troubles, had been left long unsettled. All these circumstances made it necessary for him to come to America, and tho' he made two voyages home between 1787 and 1792, he found that his permanent residence here was indispensable, and in February of the latter year he embarked for Boston with my mother, my two sisters, and myself, then ten years of age.

The family mansion in Battery March St., built after the great fire of 1760, and still firmer than most modern houses, escaped confiscation, as my grandmother, being a widow, had a life interest in it and the republicans had respect to the widow and the orphan. The house being very much out of repair, Mr. Charles Vaughan kindly invited my father to bring his family to his house till his own could be put in order, which occupied 5 or 6 weeks. My father had held a very unpopular office, but he had performed its duties with so much forbearance as to create no ill feelings towards himself, and on his return he was received in the most friendly manner by his old acquaintance; several of them, forgetting the time that had passed since they played together as boys, addressed him by the old familiar name of Bob. My mother had left England with great regret. At Bristol she was surrounded by many of her early friends, exiles like herself, with whom she could converse upon their early pleasures, and they could sympathize together upon their common misfortunes. Two of her husband's sisters were her near neighbors, and her sister Browne resided part of the year at Bristol, and during 14 years residence she had formed an agreeable circle of acquaintance among the permanent residents. In returning to her native town she came to a land of strangers, where she found very few whom she had formerly known. She missed also the conveniences of her English home, where there are so many things to lessen the labours of a mistress of a family, and during the two years that she survived, she still continued to feel as if in a foreign land.

CHAPTER 4

SCHOOLING

My father removed to the family mansion in Boston as soon as it was repaired and put in order, and I was sent to the public Latin school kept by Master Hunt. Hunt was wholly incompetent for the situation, and tho' this was well known to the public and to the school committee, he was kept there from a mistaken notion of compassion. Gentlemen did not seem to realize that to save a small tax upon their purse for his support they were sacrificing the instruction of their children in the most important years of their lives.

The following year I was taken from this school and sent to Phillips Academy, Andover, of which Mr. Pemberton, an excellent instructor, was master. The class in which I was placed was large and was soon after divided, and I was put in the lower section, being told that it was because I was not acquainted with the grammar used in the school. I felt that injustice had been done me and that I was fully equal to those in the upper division. My section was put into Ovid's Metamorphoses, and we were told that we might get as long a lesson as we chose. I studied intensely, and when we were called up to recite, I had learnt three or four times as much as any other in the section, and after being very closely examined, and found to have learnt the whole perfectly, was immediately transferred to the upper section. Mr. Pemberton, tho' an excellent man himself, could neither change the habits of the people nor liberalize their minds. The great and universal want of cleanliness was disgusting to boys brought up in respectable families, and the extreme puritan bigotry of the people was very unfavorable to the cause of religion. On Sunday we were required to commit to memory one of Watt's hymns, to be repeated at school on Monday morning. Four of us occupied a small chamber with a sanded floor, without curtains or blinds, and fronting the south west. One Sunday afternoon we left our chamber, intensely heated by the summer sun, and went into the orchard to learn our hymn under the shade of the trees. For thus desecrating the Sabbath, the old man, Timothy Abbott, with whom we boarded, rated us as if we had been guilty of felony, and threatened that if we ever again left the house on the Sabbath before the sun was down, except to go to meeting, he would complain to the master and have us expelled from the school. Owing to the want of cleanliness in the place, the boys were seldom free from cutaneous diseases. This, united to coarse fare and salt provisions and heavy bread, seriously injured my health, for I had been accustomed to delicate treatment and great indulgence. When I came home, Dr. Jeffries was consulted and gave it as his opinion that I would not regain my health so long as I remained at Andover. I was accordingly taken home, retaining like most persons who had been educated there, a rooted dislike to the place. My brother-in-law, William Tudor, had been at the same school, and his aversion to the place was quite as strong as mine. After getting away from Andover, I avoided passing through the town for very many years, and when at length I drove through it with my family, I felt a sort of surprise that it had green fields and spreading trees like other places in the world.

Upon leaving Andover, my cousin, the Rev. Dr. Gardiner, assistant minister of Trinity Church, Boston, offered to be my instructor in the classics, and I went regularly to him for some months to recite the lessons I had learnt at home. He was a very fine classical scholar, probably at that time the best in the United States, having been himself the pupil of the celebrated Dr. Parr. He possessed uncommon power of exciting the minds of young men. He subsequently kept a large day school, where the pupils became distinguished for their classical attainments. He united great strictness with great indulgence, and provided the boys would thoroughly learn their lessons, he allowed them great liberty, but he used the rattan very freely on delinquents, and in the midst of any talking and noise in the school, the lifting up of the Dr.'s finger would produce immediate silence. I have ever considered it a great misfortune that I did not continue under his instruction, but my father got the impression that I was wasting my time because the Dr. would play battledore with me after I had finished my task. At home I said nothing about my lessons, but only how long we had kept up the shuttlecock. I was therefore taken from the Dr.'s instruction and sent to school at Hingham.

The preceptor of Derby Academy at the time was Abner Lincoln, a relative and son in law of Genl. Lincoln, distinguished in the war of the revolution. He was said to have been at one time a good master, but he had so long indulged in intemperate habits as to be incapacitated for his duties, which he neglected the greater part of the three years I was there at school; the latter part of the time laying his head on the desk and going to sleep. Hingham formed a strong contrast to Andover. The dark spirit of puritanism did not brood over the fields of Hingham, and the people were sufficiently refined not to tolerate that excessive want of cleanliness so productive of discomfort and disease at the former place. The discipline of the school was lax, and there was no supervision of the boys out of the school room. In the summer time, we were generally allowed on Saturday to recite our lessons as soon as learnt and to get excused from school by 10 or 11 o'clock in the forenoon, and taking a luncheon with us, we rambled to the neighboring villages or to Nantasket beach, and sometimes over the beach to the town of Hull. We were unrestrained in our sports, many of which were attended with considerable danger. Sometimes we hired a large sail boat to visit neighboring islands, and having little knowledge of its management, were exposed to considerable danger. Towards the end of winter one of our amusements was to cut out large cakes of ice, and with long poles move round the mill pond or shallow harbour. Indulging in this sport, I once came very near being drowned; while I was cutting out a cake I fell thru' the ice where the water was deep, and there was no one within hearing. In endeavoring to extricate myself I broke away the ice till I came to where it was strong enough to bear my weight, when I got out without assistance. Another of our dangerous sports was to swim through floodgates which admitted the tide to fill a large mill pond. The current was very strong, and one boy lost his life by striking the centre post. Many other of our sports were attended with danger, and though accidents occurred, they were very rarely fatal, and the experience, caution, and self command that we acquired, were a full equivalent to the risk we incurred.

During the first year that I was at Hingham I lost my mother by consumption. She was a most fond and kind parent, and doted upon me, her only son. The ill effects of her excessive indulgence were counteracted by the levelling spirit of a public school, where no fastidious consequence can exist, and where boys soon lose the self-importance they may have brought from home. My mother had imbibed strong religious principles from her father, which she instilled into her children, who all regarded her with warm affection. What faults I might have committed or mischief I might have done, I never received a harsh word from her or from my father. My sister Hannah had imbibed the seeds of the same insidious disease, and followed her mother to the tomb in less than three months. Hannah was endowed by nature with a most lovely disposition. She had considerable personal beauty, a well cultivated mind and that natural sweetness of temper which endeared her to all who knew her, and prepossessed strangers in her favour.

Anne had neither the personal attractions nor the uncommon loveliness of disposition of her sister, but she possessed good temper, good sense, and good principles, and grief for the loss of her mother and sister had loosened her attachments to the world and strengthened her love to God.

After the loss of her mother and sister she gave up in a great degree general society, and devoted herself to making her father's home comfortable and nurturing in me the seeds of piety which had been already sown. Owing to my being at school at Hingham she could not be with me as much as she wished. In the summers of 1795 and 1796, instead of accompanying my father to Kennebec, she, with her maid, took lodgings at Hingham that she might be near to watch over me, and after school hours I was in the habit of walking with her or reading religious books to her, while she plied her needle.

Though naturally of a strong constitution, yet the almost entire seclusion from society and brooding over her own grief gradually undermined her health, and she at length fell a victim to the same disease which had terminated the lives of her mother and sister six years previously.

The boys of Derby Academy were mostly from wealthy families living in Boston, but had been subject at home to very little moral discipline, and, to the mischievous propensities so common to undisciplined school boys added vices of a more mature age. It was unfortunate that I should have been placed among such associates, but the religious feelings which I had imbibed from my mother and sister saved me from joining in their worst excesses, and without exciting their hostility I could occasionally point out to them the impropriety of their conduct and fortify what I said with texts of scripture.

As a child, I had been troubled with stuttering, and at school it was sometimes a minute or more before I could get the word out that I wished, and then not till my face had become red and swollen, but by taking pains in my utterance and changing a word I could not pronounce, I gradually surmounted the difficulty and have never again been troubled with it.

It may not be irrevelant here to refer to the French Revolution, which so strongly agitated the whole country and extended its influence even to boys at school. That revolution, which uprooted the fabric of French society from its very base, was hailed by many enthusiasts in England as the harbinger of universal freedom, but in this country with what seemed a universal burst of delight. Our self esteem was flattered that it was from our example that that volatile nation had exchanged a monarchical for a republican form of government and had thus been enabled to strike off the chains of a feudal despotism that had for many centuries crushed the energies of the people. It was thought that the dreams of the French philosophers were about to be realized. That the liberty and equality which they had inscribed on all their public edifices were to spread throughout the world and as its consequence produce universal happiness. Demonstrations of sympathy were everywhere exhibited. In Boston the triumph of French liberty was celebrated by what was termed a civic feast. An ox which had been several days roasting whole was carried to State St., where tables were spread its whole length for the feast. It was followed in procession by the municipal authorities, public officers, the various societies and trades, and the schools, every one wearing the French cockade.

There was not room for the school children at the tables, but we were all treated with a cake of gingerbread with the cabalistic words, liberty and equality, impressed upon it. The company did not find the ox very palatable, and they soon began to amuse themselves by pelting with it the spectators in the balconies around.

The horns of the ox were gilt and placed on a liberty pole in Liberty Square, but this universal rejoicing was soon checked by the successive arrivals from France. Governments there had been overthrown in rapid succession till the reins of power were seized by the remorseless Jacobins, who perpetrated deeds of violence and barbarity which the strongest testimony scarcely makes credible.

As soon as it was known that the feeble Louis XVI, the most unoffending of his race, had been brought to the scaffold for the sins of his predecessors, a strong reaction everywhere took place.

The Federal party, which embraced almost all the persons of wealth and education of the country and a large proportion of the officers who had effected our independence, now began to fear lest the constitutional edifice which they had taken such pains to rear and to consolidate should be overthrown in the turmoil. They desired to put a stop to this effervescence of popular feeling. They had the ox horns draped with the emblems of mourning for the death of the King, the flag on liberty pole lowered to half mast, but the French sympathies were not to be so checked. They insisted upon the crepe being taken off the horns and the flag hoisted to its full height. Amid the noise and violence of the disputants, a man went into the dock, it being low water, and cut off the pole at the base, and the pole with all upon it fell into the mud. It thus being made a drawn game, they dispersed.

Parties became more and more embittered against each other. All social intercourse between them ceased. Forgetting that they were Americans, they identified themselves as English or French partisans, placing on their hats the emblematic cockade of one or the other nation. The streets everywhere resounded with the French national songs of ça ira or carmagnole or else with dogrel rhymes, denouncing the English and praising the French. The people were excited against the English by being reminded of what they had suffered from them during the revolutionary struggle, and the mob burnt at the Long Wharf an English letter of marque from Bermuda, loaded with pineapples. The instigators kept in the background, and a painter was arrested and punished for the offence. Another act of violence was attempted against a Jew named Wallack, who was unpopular for his anti-Gallican sentiments. He kept an armourer's shop. The mob threatened the house and would have gutted it and seized the arms and probably illtreated the owner, had not a party of gentlemen volunteered to defend the house, and for several nights kept watch with a cannon loaded with grape, which effectually deterred the mob.

Genet, the French Minister to this country, taking advantage of this state of feeling, exerted himself to drive this country into a war with England and alliance with France, and for this purpose issued letters of marque and reprisal against British commerce. Many French had fled from the negro insurrection in St. Domingo and leaving their property behind, had sought an asylum here. Some of these readily accepted these letters, as while it offered them the means of obtaining property, it gratified their national antipathy to England. Washington, alive to the evils which a war with Great Britain would inflict upon the country, scarcely recovered from the effects of the revolutionary struggle, issued his proclamation of neutrality, thus saving us from being drawn into the vortex of European politics, tho' he was fully aware of the extreme unpopularity of the measure with the great mass of people. Genet, the French Minister, undertook to appeal to them against the President. Washington had the firmness to demand from the French Government the recall of Genet, and he was sustained by the conservative portions of the community. This strong party spirit was not confined to the mature members of the community but descended to boys at school.

At Hingham every boy mounted a cockade, the colour denoting the party with which were his predelictions. All the boys but one other and myself mounted the tricoloured cockade. We put the black in our hats. This we were, of course, not allowed to do peaceably, and the odds being so greatly against us they were defended with difficulty, but when forcibly taken from us we were readily supplied with new ones by the Miss Barbers with whom we boarded and who were strong tories.

This fostered a spirit of independence which had its influence on my future character. In another instance of minor importance I braved the jeers of my companions by wearing till I entered college the costume of an English school boy, long coat and breeches. For this I was not only laughed at by my school fellows but when in Boston had to bear the assaults of under boys, in defending myself from whom I received occasionally a bloody nose. A nonconformity to the customs of the world in things of no importance in themselves, such as the fashion of dress, is certainly no mark of wisdom, but in my case it aided to strengthen the spirit of independence.

CHAPTER 5

HARVARD COLLEGE

In 1797 I left Hingham and entered Harvard College. At my examination I was so much agitated as scarcely to be able to answer the questions proposed, although I had been fully prepared to enter for a year previously. During my freshman year I chummed with a worthy young man by the name of Abbot. Our tastes and sympathies were wholly different, yet we lived in harmony till he was obliged to leave college from incipient consumption, which terminated fatally and never allowed him to return. The custom of fagging, brought from the schools of the old country, had not become so obselete when I entered college but that it was thought necessary for each freshman to choose a particular senior whose written order for any trifling service exempted him from the claim of any other member of the college. I selected Thomas Welsh, who afterwards went as private secretary to John Quincy Adams when appointed minister to Berlin. The custom, however, had got so much into disuse that my order was never shown. I had been but a few weeks in college when Welsh invited me to a large supper party in his room, where a long table was covered with abundance of poultry. In my simplicity I had no suspicion that the feast had not been honestly procured in the market, but I soon learnt that forages in the neighboring poultry yards and gardens were not uncommon, but neither myself nor any of my friends were concerned in these raids. At this supper I smoked my first cigar which I found very disagreeable, making me sick, but companionship induced me to smoke occasionally afterwards while in college. After my return from Europe, joining a club of inveterate smokers, I fell into the same habit, but my betrothed said to me one evening that she wished I did not smoke. I made no reply, but have not smoked since.

The landlady with whom I boarded in my freshman year

was in reduced circumstances and endeavored to eke out her income by stinting her boarders in food. The next year I took lodgings at Miss Chadbourn's, where we had every thing comfortable, and I continued there thro' my college course, never having lived in the college buildings or boarded in commons. Judge Winthrop took his meals at the same place, living alone in his own large house opposite. He had been librarian to the College for many years, and, as he was a good mathematician, he expected on the death of his father to have succeeded him in the mathematical chair, but his intemperate habits prevented his election. This deeply mortified him. He immediately resigned the office of librarian and determined that this habit should never again interfere with his success in life. For this purpose he placed on one side of his study table a bottle of brandy and glass, and on the other, pipes and tobacco and in front, a bible. He felt with the temptation always in sight, and the bible as an antidote, he would never be surprised into yielding to the temptation. As a stimulus he substituted hot water at his meals for ardent spirits. After a year of this discipline he felt that he had acquired so much self-command as to be able to dispense with these mementoes which were then removed. I occasionally accepted an invitation to sit with him after dinner in his study, and he always offered me a glass of wine, and he was able to take one himself without its recalling his taste for strong drinks, tho' he never took wine when alone. He employed much time on a work on the Book of Revelations, applying them to the current events of the day, but like many abler men, he lived to see events falsify his expectations.

There were several societies in college which had been instituted many years previously and had been transmitted from class to class. Some of these were exclusively literary, and some social. Of most of them I was a member, but our social pleasure was principally derived from a coffee club formed from our classmates in our freshman year. Soon after its formation we perceived that two of our number were not congenial with the majority. We therefore dissolved the club and reconstituted it the next day, leaving out the two that did not harmonize with the rest of us. Our club then consisted of Dawes, Forester, Gorham, Bant Sullivan and his brother George, Nat. Williams, and myself. We met regularly during our whole college course once a week in a small back room in Porter's tavern, where we had for supper beefsteak and coffee, without wine or spirits, and for which we paid a quarter of a dollar each. Our evenings passed very pleasantly, closing at about 11 o'clock. I do not recollect that any thing ever occurred to disturb the harmony of the meetings. Occasionally we had pleasantry and songs, but usually discussions on important subjects, sometimes on questions beyond our depth, and occasionally on questions that the ablest philosophers have failed to solve. Our club was a little exclusive, and we were called aristocratic, notwithstanding which we were on good terms with our fellow students, and, as we had the character of good fellows, we were ambitious of being good scholars, and were so far successful that I had the 2nd part on graduating, Williams and G. Sullivan the 3rd and 4th, and all the others respectable parts, save only one.

Early in my senior year Jas. Bartlet a lawyer residing at Cambridge, a man plausible but utterly unprincipled, called on me several times, being very civil and giving me urgent invitations to his house. I was aware of his design, which was to inveigle me, as he had other scholars into card playing and to get from me all the money I had or could obtain from my friends. I resisted all his invitations and solicitations, and then he wrote me bullying letters, of which I took no notice. Soon after, I had the English oration at the fall exhibition, and Bartlet published in the Boston Chronicle a critique on the performance calling it the firefly of genius and the effervescence of art. My classmate, Tim. Fuller, father of Madame D'Ossoli, answered Bartlet in the next Chronicle, which was the more generous in him as I did not belong to his set, and as he had expected himself the oration, which was given to me. Bartlet afterwards removed into Maine and settled at Saco, where he built a house which he made remarkable by painting it black. He became there notorious for every species of low pettyfogging, and was continually either a plaintiff or defendant in actions of slander. He sued the printer of the Portland

Advertiser for defamation. This was a warm federal paper, and the cause coming before a democratic jury, he obtained a verdict in his favour with large damages, which the printer being unable to pay, he went to jail, giving bonds for the liberty of the yard. By the law as it then stood, debtors having the liberty of the yard had a large range in the day time, but at night were obliged to confine themselves to the precincts of the prison. The pump was just without these precincts, and Bartlet kept a man to watch the jail, who one evening perceived the printer filling his pitcher at the pump after the prescribed hour for his retirement, and Bartlet recovered of the bondsmen double the amount of the verdict.

The instruction at Harvard at that period was in the school boy style, not equal to what is now found in many of our high schools. In the classics we were only taught to construe into such English as would give the literal meaning of the author without any attention to the depth and elevation of his thoughts or the beauty of his language. I stood high in my class in mathematics, and yet I knew nothing of fluxions or of algebra, beyond simple equations. In history we were only taught to commit to memory certain facts and dates, and the only book we studied in metaphysics was Locke on the Understanding. Yet at that time Harvard had a higher reputation than any college in the Union.

The three upper classes were instructed one day in the week in theology by Dr. Tappan, the professor of divinity, from a textbook by Doddridge, in which religious truth was sought to be proved by the geometrical formula, which led us to expect the same certainty that we found in our mathematics, where certain results follow from assumed data and no other can be drawn from them, but ethics do not admit of similar proof. Writers upon the subject are not even agreed upon the fundamental principles upon which their doctrines should be based. Disappointed in not finding the certainty which the use of mathematical forms had led us to expect, we began to doubt the truth of what we were taught, till we gradually lapsed into scepticism. If our professor perceived the unhappy state of mind into which we were gradually subsiding, he took no pains to check it and remove our doubts. All he required of us was to give the views of our author, without any enquiry whether we fully comprehended them and acquiesced in their truth.

Professor Pearson had Bishop Watson's "Address to Young Persons after Confirmation" omitting some passages relating to the rite, printed at his own expense, and distributed gratuitously to all the scholars. It is well adapted to produce a strong impression on the minds of young men. I read it several times with great attention, nor has my opinion of its value been altered by a very recent perusal, but being addressed to those who had just renewed their baptismal vows, it took for granted the truth of the Christian system, and therefore had no relation to the doubts created in our mind by our theological studies. A spirit of scepticism was prevailing in the college. French philosophy with its infidelity had become popular.

The writers of that school, particularly Rousseau, were read and admired, without their fallacy being perceived. Their sentiments were freely discussed in our club, particularly the doctrine of suicide. Bant Sullivan, one of our class, a man of warm and generous feelings, always supported its lawfulness, saying that as we were brought into the world without our consent, there was no obligation upon us to remain longer than it was agreeable, and he unhappily acted upon that opinion some years subsequently. He always kept loaded pistols in his room, and in a moment of disappointment, evidently with very little premeditation, he put an end to his existence in the 25th year of his age.

In my sophomore year I lived alone, and the latter part of my junior year. In the former part of it William Paine, a nephew of Mrs. James Perkins, shared my room. He was a young man of excellent character, fine abilities, and a most remarkable memory, for whom I felt a warm friendship. He left college in the middle of his junior year to enter the countinghouse of Messrs. James and T. H. Perkins. He won the entire confidence of those gentlemen, and they proposed that he should go out to Canton to reside as their agent and partner in business, a situation to which Mr. John

Cushing succeeded, and where he acquired his very large fortune.

Paine hesitated long before he accepted the tempting proposal, frequently reasoning with me upon the subject, questioning if it was worth while to sacrifice ten of the best years of life among semi-barbarians to acquire a fortune which, when obtained, the power of enjoying might be lost. He finally resolved on the sacrifice and accepted the offer. But the certain expectation of the fortune proved fallacious. Paine had not been more than three or four years at Canton before our government commenced that course of commercial restrictions, embargo and non-intercourse which, terminating in war, destroyed all legitimate commerce. Tired of remaining at Canton doing nothing, he relinquished his connection with the Messrs. Perkins and removed to the Isle of France and established himself there in business. But his prospects were again blighted by the transfer of the island to the British. He then removed to Batavia, where he died, never having again revisited his native country. He left a moderate fortune, which he bequeathed to a Dutch lad saved from a shipwrecked vessel, whom he had adopted and taken into his counting room. Tho' our friendship was sincere, yet from the difficulty of transmitting letters we kept up no correspondence after he had left for Canton. When my relative, Capt. Dumaresq, was at Batavia, he sent me by him a collection of engravings of the native chiefs of the island of Java as a reminiscence. He is an instance of the truth of the words of the wise king of Israel that, 'riches are not to men of understanding, nor yet favour to men of skill, but time and chance happeneth to them all.'

His disappointments arose from circumstances which could not be foreseen and over which he could have no control. Had he remained at home and entered a profession, he must have become distinguished and would in all human probability have done honour to his country.

John Gorham was my chum in my senior year, and we formed a friendship which continued uninterrupted till he was called to the world of spirits in his 47th year. He had a warm heart and prepossessing manners. He held a respectable standing in the class, though not distinguished as a scholar. Upon graduating he commenced the study of medicine with Dr. Warren, then at the head of the profession in Mass., and whose daughter he subsequently married.

While completing his medical education in Edinburgh the failure of his father occurred, which had an important bearing upon his future character. His agreeable manners and social disposition, with his musical taste, made him a general favorite, and there was great danger that the attractions of social intercourse would have driven him off from those studies which were essential to success in his profession, but after he was thrown wholly on his own resources, he laid aside his flute and gave up all company but that of a few cherished friends, and devoted himself to his profession. As it is a slow process for a young physician to get into good practice, in order to increase his income he gave for some years an annual course of popular lectures on chemistry, which, beside the emolument, gave him reputation, and he was soon after appointed professor of chemistry at Harvard. He published a work on that science in two octavo volumes, which had considerable reputation, and was adopted as a textbook in several colleges, but the rapid advance of the science soon put it out of date, and his practice as a physician had so much increased as not to allow time to prepare a revised edition. It obliged him also to give up his public lectures, the emolument of which he no longer needed, and subsequently his professorship. At the time of his death he had a large practice among the first families in Boston.

He had warm friends, and his loss was not only mourned by them, but by his numerous patients to whom his medical skill, his close attention to them in sickness, and his kind and very pleasant manners greatly endeared him. In the vacation immediately before leaving college he came down and spent some weeks with me in Kennebec, and in company with Wm. C. Wilde and Wm. O. Vaughan we took a journey on horseback to the Penobscot and stopping at Thomaston we spent 4 or 5 days at Genl. Knox's.

At the time I was in college it was customary for the

parents of those young men who had parts at commencement to give entertainment to their friends. When I graduated, my father, partly for my honour, and partly to return civilities that he had received, gave a more splendid entertainment than had ever previously been given. He hired a large house, in addition to which he had a marquee erected under the trees in the garden, where Dr. Gardiner presided. The entertainment was got up under the direction of Vilor, who was directed to have everything of the best kind, and who was then noted for providing the best suppers of any one in Boston. I have been reminded of the elegance and the good cheer of the occasion by persons who had partaken of it more than a half century previous.

I kept up an intimate intercourse and frequent correspondence with several of our club for a number of years after we graduated, and with one, Nathaniel Williams, a most excellent fellow, for many years in public life, either as U. S. district attorney for the State of Maryland, or as a member of one or other branch of the legislature of that State, I still keep up a very friendly correspondence. Thirty four only were graduated in our class, and after a period of sixty years, eight of them had not the fatal mark of death attached to their names in the college catalogue.

During the whole of my college course I spent my summer vacations at Kennebec. My father came down to attend to the Cobbossee estate and he had built on the Worromontogus stream opposite the village of Gardiner a cottage in which he resided and which I continued to occupy till I removed in 1810 to the mansion I had built at Oaklands.

CHAPTER 6

ENGLISH COUSINS

Immediately after taking my degree, my name was entered as a student at law in the office of Mr. John Lowell, and I went to spend the summer in Kennebec. My health had been delicate from infancy, and it was feared that the same disease which had carried off my mother and sisters was commencing its ravages upon me. Instead, therefore, of going into a lawyer's office I was advised to travel in Europe till I should attain my majority, when my presence would be necessary here. Unfortunately, I was not prepared for foreign travel. I could read French but was unable to speak any language but my native tongue, and I had little knowledge of the literature, manners, or customs of continental Europe. My letters of introduction were only to merchants and might be considered merely as bills of exchange for a dinner. And tho' I became acquainted in England with a few country gentlemen and their families, this acquaintance was quite limited, and I was introduced to no literary or scientific society. I went to England with the family of Mr. Dickerson, an English merchant who had made a large fortune in this country, to which he had become attached, and would not have left it but for the urgent solicitations of his father.

On my arrival I went immediately to Mr. Wm. Vaughan's,* who kept bachelor's hall in London. He received me into his house in the most friendly manner and after a few days

*Note of R. H. G. 2nd.

Father used to tell us that when he first arrived in London and was staying with Mr. William Vaughan, he suggested to Mr. V. that as he had two or three months at his command, he would like to go into his counting room and learn bookkeeping. Mr. V. answered "learn bookkeeping in three months! why you could not think of doing it under seven years, and that would be scarcely time enough." And to this father added to us the remark, Mr. Vaughan kept five distinct sets of books, and contrived to bookkeep away the whole of his own and the family estates, and died a bankrupt.

despatched me to his mother, my aunt, who spent part of the year at Brighton with her aged husband and two unmarried daughters. She had a fine understanding and great dignity of character, and that Christian kindness and courtesy which are superior to all artificial polish of manners, and was strongly endued with that most useful of all qualities, common sense.

I arrived there at tea time and was received with the cordiality to be expected for the only son of a beloved brother. After many enquiries about my health and habits, finding that I did not wear flannel, without saying anything to me on the subject, she had a suit made up that evening and placed at my bed side ready to put on in the morning. Mrs. Darby, the oldest daughter of Mrs. Vaughan, was staying at the same time at Brighton with some of her children, and I there first became acquainted with them. Mr. Darby belonged to an Irish aristocratic family possessed of valuable estates, but as a younger son he was without fortune. Disregarding the prejudices of his class he established himself in London as a merchant, and from his own character and the standing of the family, he became the principal agent of the extensive linen manufacturers in the neighborhood of the family estates and acquired a handsome fortune. He had a family of eight children, with several of whom I subsequently became intimate.

When I was staying with them at my aunt's at Hackney, I formed a particular friendship with Susan, the oldest daughter, an uncommonly fine woman, who subsequently married Mr. Pennyfether, an eminent Irish barrister, who became Chief Justice of Ireland with the title of Baron Pennyfether. The oldest son, Jonathan, was a young man of most excellent character but died soon after I left England. Mr. Darby's oldest brother, an Admiral in the British navy, was never married, and upon his death the extensive Irish estates descended to Mr. Darby's son, William Henry, being then the oldest. He had joined a set of fanatics called the Plymouth Brethren or Darbyites. By their principles they eschewed all the luxuries and even comforts of life, had all things in common, and dressed in the plainest and coarsest clothes. Upon becoming entitled to these estates, he relinquished them to a younger brother, only stipulating for an annuity of £1000 per annum, which he appropriated to the common use of all the brethren in the faith. The sect do not admit that any ministry was established by Christ, but believe that the gift of the Holy Spirit is poured equally upon all his disciples, and that all are equally bound to administer to the bodily and spiritual wants of their fellow beings, disregarding all ties of kindred, and preaching the gospel to every creature. Acting upon these principles he gave up all intercourse with his family, not even calling, as he passed thru London, to see his mother. The sect, I believe, is still in existence.

Of Mr. Vaughan's two daughters residing at the time with their parents, the oldest, Sarah, had not only the benevolence and kindness which were the ruling traits of the family, but made it the sole principle of her life. She did not hesitate to say that she had acted fully up to this principle and therefore considered herself entitled to future blessedness. We became well acquainted with her when she resided with her brother Benjamin.

After spending a few weeks at Brighton, I returned to London and thence for the winter to Bristol, where my father's two sisters Gould and Bishop, both widows, resided. Mrs. Gould had been distinguished in her youth for her beauty. We had a portrait of her painted by Copley as Diana, which was unfortunately lost when my father removed from the family mansion. When I knew her she had still a commanding person and very dignified manners, a fine mind, sharp wit and great powers of sarcasm, tho' she was at the same time quite religious. Her husband died at Gibraltar of consumption and, from a mistaken notion of honor, would not sell out his commission with a mortal disease upon him. His father had cut him off in his will for marrying in America, but when my aunt became known to her husband's family, she acquired their respect and esteem, and her brother in law settled an annuity upon her which enabled her to keep a genteel establishment, and live with perfect comfort. She had one only daughter, of whom I

MRS. ARTHUR BROWNE

By Copley

shall speak hereafter. Her sister Bishop, also a widow, had lodgings in the same street, but she had neither the understanding or dignified manners of Mrs. Gould. I had been some weeks at the hot well before I learned that my mother's sister Browne resided in the same street within a few doors of my lodgings. She had also been very beautiful in her youth and had taken unconceived pains to preserve her good looks. When I knew her, her person had become clumsy, but she was still handsome, and tho' she must have been over 60, she did not appear 40. She formed a strong contrast both in appearance and manners to my aunt Gould. Rank, fashion and wealth were the chief objects of her admiration. She had a good deal of arrogance and had exacted from her husband's connections an attention and deference which were voluntarily paid to my aunt Gould by the relations of her husband. Her husband was the second son of the Earl of Altamont, and she had placed a very exaggerated value upon the factitious distinctions of rank and fortune. I did not see her sons, who were in the army. Her two daughters had been educated to consider rank and station in fashionable society as the most desirable objects in life. They had been frequent visitants to their aristocratic connections in Dublin. The youngest had been a guest at the Lord Lieutenant's at the time of the great rebellion in 1798. She told me that at the castle and at the houses of the principal gentry the lower half of the windows on the ground apartments were blocked up with brick or stone to prevent being fired upon by the rebels, and they never sat down to table without the gentlemen having loaded pistols by the side of their plates to defend themselves in case of any sudden attack. Such is civil war.

I met at the public rooms and at my Aunt Browne's a Mrs. Sheers, the widow of a distinguished barrister who had been engaged in the rebellion. He and one brother were taken with arms in their hands, and were tried and executed for treason. Two other brothers, while attempting to escape after the defeat, were drowned. The loss of four sons, men of talent and accomplishment, in the course of a few days, produced a deep grief in the mother, which, though it did not immediately destroy the vital spark, left it all but extinguished. She took to her bed and never after left it. Not so with the widow I knew, who, tho' she still wore her weeds, went constantly into society, with a gaiety contrasting strongly with her former history.

The physician whom I consulted in London had advised my spending the winter at the hot wells at Bristol and in the spring go to the still milder climate of Devonshire. He also told me that it was necessary for my health not to study or read in the evening. I therefore joined my aunt Browne in her card parties, which took place almost every evening. The favourite game was casino, which was played for a moderate stake. I kept a purse specially for the card table, and I found its contents at the end of the winter differed but little from its state at the beginning, but though the stake played for was small, it was sufficient to excite bad temper, and titled ladies in their anger scrupled not to take their maker's name in vain. I became a very good player at casino and at whist but when I found subsequently that in Boston, as well as in England people could not restrain their temper when luck was against them, I determined to give up playing cards altogether. I had also become too fond of them, and I have never had them in my house. Manners have now so much improved that, when there is not the stimulus of gain, cards are frequently played in a social way without bad passions being exhibited.

Early in March I left Bristol for Devonshire, where I passed between 3 and 4 months very pleasantly. I had a few good letters of introduction, which gave me a general acquaintance with the gentry of the country, whom I found extremely agreeable and hospitable. I was here first introduced to the charm of English country life, where the pleasures of society are enjoyed without its restraints. In every instance pains were taken to make my visit agreeable, and I was introduced to the neighbouring gentry. The climate of Devonshire is so mild that the bay, the laurel and the myrtle grow and retain their foliage through the winter in the open air, and the grass continuing green, you are scarcely reminded that it is elsewhere the season of ice and snow.

In June I returned to Bristol and spent a fortnight with my Aunt Gould. She was kind, but extremely precise, and not disposed to allow the slightest deviation from the formal rules of propriety which she had adopted.

Having been advised to take exercise on horseback, I bought a horse at Bristol and spent a couple of months rambling among the mountains of Wales. I was so thin that my bones came thro' my skin, but I gradually gained flesh and strength. Gentlemen seldom travel in England on horseback without a servant, and I found it awkward to be without one when I stopped at houses where I had letters of introduction. I met the Aiken family in my rambles, distinguished for their literary and scientific pursuits, and travelled with them several days, finding them very agreeable, tho' they belonged to the Utilitarian school. I had a letter of introduction to a clergyman who was very particular in his enquiries about the church in this country. He was disgusted at the idea of a clergyman's being dependent for his support upon the voluntary contributions of his people, and could scarcely believe that any respectable clergyman could so degrade himself.

On the main roads I found English generally spoken, but in the less frequented parts it was little used, the vernacular Welch prevailing. The men usually understood English, but the women and children only their native tongue. In some churches English was used in the morning and Welsh in the afternoon, but at that time there were but few of the clergy of the Episcopal Church acquainted with Welsh, and the Methodists, by preaching in their native tongue, made many converts. Some of the bishops recently appointed are able to address the people in Welsh, and require that their clergy should do the same, and are thus bringing back to the fold some of the sheep that had strayed away. There was much that was interesting in my tour. Berkeley Castle, where Edward 2d was murdered, is still kept in its pristine order with the original furniture preserved. There is a small garden on the top of one of its towers, with fruit trees in bearing. I then proceeded towards the mountains, of which Snowden is the highest (3567 ft.), and almost always enveloped in clouds. I remained at its foot a week, hoping in vain for an opportunity to see the extensive prospect from its summit.

Conway Castle is a very singular ruin. One of its towers, which rested on a slate quarry, has been undermined and the lower half fallen, while the upper part remains, adhering to the wall of the castle by the strength of its cement. The slate quarries of Wales are very extensive, supplying a large portion of the United States as well as many parts of Europe. The copper mines of Anglesea, being situated on sterile soil, are said to have been given by the aristocratic owner as a valueless dower to his daughter, who had married against his consent to a poor clergyman, whom it made very wealthy.

Leaving Wales, I passed by Liverpool and thro' the northern manufacturing districts, stopping long enough at each place to see what was interesting. At Nontwich I descended into the salt mines. Sitting in a workman's lap I was lowered in a bucket to a great depth. The crude salt is boiled to drive off the impurities and is then crystallized. In Staffordshire I saw a great number of neatly dressed young women employed in painting china, but the work is now, I believe, done with blocks.

In my journey I spent a day at Cheltenham, a fashionable watering place, but very uninteresting. It is there the duty of the master of ceremonies to call upon all strangers who enter their names on the books, and find them partners in the dance or at the card table, according to their taste. I never saw people appear to lead a more wearisome life than did the company there, some of whom came for the benefit of the waters, which are said to have valuable medicinal properties, others only *"pour passer le temps."*

I was unfortunate in finding, when I reached Oxford, that the vacation had commenced, and that the gentlemen to whom I had letters being absent, I could only see what a guide could point out.

Upon my return to London I spent some weeks among my relations in the vicinity of that city. At my Aunt Vaughan's, I renewed my intimacy with the Darbys, one or more of the children being constantly with their grandmother. With Jonathan, a young man of high principle and with Susan, afterwards Mrs. Pennyfether, I became on the most friendly terms.

I passed a few days with Admiral Hallowell, possessing all the fine traits of a naval officer. He was on intimate terms with the persecuted wife of the Prince Regent, dining there frequently. She had not them become notorious, but was considered only as an ill treated and injured woman.

With Mrs. Gee, the only child of my Aunt Gould I spent a week. Mrs. Gee had been educated with great care by her mother, and to a good person added a fine understanding and excellent principles. In her youth she and her cousin Benjamin, now Admiral Hallowell, had been strongly and mutually attached, but marriage was out of the question, he being only a poor lieutenant and she dependent upon her mother, who, having only a life annuity, could make no provision for her. She therefore became very anxious to see her daughter comfortably established before she herself should be called away, and persuaded her to accept an offer of marriage from a Mr. Gee, a wealthy bachelor, but old enough to be her father. He was one of the remaining fox hunting squires who by the tenure of his estate was obliged to keep a pack of hounds, but the habits of that class had been gradually changing, and Mr. Gee conformed to the times, had twice made the grand tour of Europe, and had made himself familiar with the names of the places and hotels where the most delicious wines and greatest delicacies were to be procured, and also professed to be a connoisseur in music. When I knew him, having become corpulent, he was glad of any excuse not to be obliged to follow the chase. He had great regard for the superior understanding of his wife, and while she showed him the respect due to the master of the family, and took pains to gratify his wishes and always to have a good table, he willingly relinquished to her the whole management of his property, of which she kept all the accounts. The rector of the parish dined with Mr. Gee once or twice a week, when they sat over their bottle till the latter fell asleep. What a trial for a clergyman to feel himself thus obliged from their relative positions and necessary intercourse thus to spend so much of his time.

The place had no natural advantage, but was laid out with much care and its gardens and shrubbery, all kept in fine order, made it a beautiful place.

The river Wandle, a brook large enough to turn some mills below, was made into cascades. The place had been famous in the time of Queen Elizabeth, who was said to have been an occasional visitor there to the Carew family, ancestors of Mr. Gee. The arrangement of the house will give an idea of the habits of mediaeval aristocratic life.

The house formed three sides of a parallelogram, the entire centre portion forming one large lofty hall used for feasting the retainers of the family, and ornamented with the trophies obtained in hunting, and the armorial bearings of the various branches of the Carew family. The rest of the house consisted of small apartments, the dining room being of very moderate size. Mr. Gee told me that it was customary on rent day, when the tenants assembled to pay their dues, that they should dine with the lord of the manor. In his youth the tenants on such occasions filled the large hall. When a better system of farming was introduced, it was found that a man with capital could afford to pay a much larger rent per acre for a great than a small farm. The consequence has been that the less intelligent and poorer tenants have been reduced to day labourers, and the number of Mr. Gee's tenants so diminished that they can all be seated in the common dining parlour.

The house, tho' of brick, was originally built with heavy buttresses, but to give it a modern appearance a regular wall had been built even with the front of the buttress, leaving a space between, forming a nice hiding place for a novelist. The whole house was wainscotted with oak, which, having turned black with age, gave it a gloomy appearance.

After I was there Mr. Gee's oldest brother, who had taken the family name of Carew, came to reside with his brother at Beddington. By his will he left all his estate to his brother Gee, and when Gee died he bequeathed all his property to his wife, and she, remembering her early attachment, left all the estate to her cousin Sir Benjamin Hallowell, upon the condition that he should add to his own name that of Carew, which had so long been connected with the

Beddington property. Not being entailed, it has been since cut up among the Admiral's descendants. It is a little remarkable that the only three grandsons of my grandfather Benjamin Hallowell who left descendants, changed their names respectively to Boylston, Carew and Gardiner, so that there is no descendant of his that now bears his name.

In London I met Mr. and Mrs. Apthorp from Boston. Mr. A. was brother of Mrs. Charles Vaughan, which had produced some intimacy in the families. They were going on to the continent, and I accepted their invitation to accompany them. We purchased an English postchaise, depending on procuring post horses on the continent. The Apthorps, though pleasant people, were not such as were profitable companions to a young man just going forth into the world. They had neither of them any literary or scientific taste, but depended upon the passing events of the hour and the transient company they might meet for the amusement of the day, without any fixed purpose in life, or thought beyond the morrow. We could all read French. Mr. A. and myself were just able to make our wants known in that language. Mrs. A., tho' she could speak the language tolerably, made terrible blunders in the idiom. We were therefore not prepared to enjoy French society even if we had had the best letters of introduction.

W went first to Holland, and after passing rapidly thro' that country and Belgium, proceeded to Paris. Napoleon was then first consul.

We spent a couple of months there, viewing the objects of most interest. The Louvre then contained the beautiful works of art which had been plundered from Italy and Flanders. The famous horses of Lysippus, which had passed from Contantinople to Venice, were adorning the gate posts of the Tuilleries. France was then in the transition state. The churches, which had been despoiled and desecrated during the frenzy of the revolution, still remained dilapidated. Mass was reestablished in the chapel of the Tuilleries, but few of the priests had returned from exile, and there was no reappearance of religion among the people. Napoleon was only beginning to make his power felt and to restore things to order from the chaos into which they had been thrown.

We had left Paris intending to spend the remainder of the winter in the south of France and in Italy, and went to Bordeaux, where Mrs. Apthorp's brother Foster was established as a merchant. There were a number of Americans in business in Bordeaux, who, being without the restraint which public opinion imposed upon them at home, and not amenable to the opinion of those among whom they were residing, indulged in a licentiousness and open profligacy shocking to the French, who are looked upon as not over strict in their moral notions. Mr. A. with myself, intended leaving Mrs. A. with her brother and proceeding to Italy. But the roads had been wholly neglected during the revolution, and the power of Napoleon had to be consolidated before he could attend to objects which, though important, were less pressing. We could not obtain post horses, and the public carriages were suspended. We were therefore obliged, to our great regret, to abandon our intention of seeing Italy. We made a little trip to the port of Cette, on the Mediterranean, by the canal of Languedoc, a mode of conveyance only adopted by the lowest class of the people, and the scenes we were obliged to witness were so disgusting that we were glad to leave it at the first opportunity that occurred.

At Nismes I saw for the first time a Grecian Temple, the *Maison Carree*. Its beautiful simplicity, of which modern imitations give but a faint idea, struck me so forcibly that I could scarcely bring myself to remove from looking at it during the day we spent there. From Bordeaux we returned to Paris, and, as I had just attained my majority, it became necessary for me to hasten back to this country.

CHAPTER 7

GARDINER ESTATE

Spending but a short time in Boston after returning from Europe, I came to Kennebec in 1803 to take possession of and manage the estate which had been bequeathed to me in my early childhood. The property had not only suffered from my long minority, and from the absence of my father in England, but also from its being entailed. My health had been so feeble from early infancy that there was little expectation that I should live to come into its possession. Of course no portion of the property could be sold, nor could any part of it be leased for a longer period than my frail life, nor would it have been prudent for my father to have made expenditures for improvements which might at any moment have passed with the land to another branch of the family.

A still greater hindrance to the prosperity of the place was the uncertainty of title arising from the production of the forged deed. Upon the death of my uncle William his brother John found among his papers the forged deed, which he had neglected to destroy. He told my mother of it, and in half a jocose way said that he meant to have it recorded and claim his share of the property. This distressed my mother, who would remonstrate with him, that, as he knew the deed to be a forgery, he would not be so dishonest as to endeavor to establish it. He would reply that property was the creature of law, and if law would give it to him, he knew of no reason why he should not take it. My mother felt, however, that he had no intention of attempting to prove the validity of the deed for it was in his possession six years, during which he did not even have it recorded, but was only meaning to tease his sister. When he died his son William found the deed among his father's papers. He had neither the talents of his father or brother but had pleasing manners and was a favorite in the society of ladies. He had been bred to no business, and had expended the patrimony he inherited from my grandfather in supporting himself as a gentleman of leisure. He was very intimate in my father's family, coming at all hours and staying without invitation. He had not the manliness to give my father any intimation of the course he intended to pursue, but had the deed recorded in the county of Kennebec where he took out letters of administration on his uncle William's estate, and the first notice he gave my father was by the sheriff serving upon him a writ of ejectment as my guardian. He was poor and the temptation was great. If he could establish the validity of the deed, of which the prospect was favorable, he would secure a comfortable maintenance for a number of years while settling the estate, and as heir would be entitled to a fifteenth of the whole property and be relieved from all his embarrassments. He had never been a man of principle, for in a will of his father's which I had in my possession till it was burnt in my office, my uncle reprobated in strong terms the conduct of his son William, and bequeathed him 'one copper with the head and superscription of that booby George the Third.' At that period coppers with the head of George the Third passed current at only half the value of those with any other British sovereign's head. The will was not executed but is in my uncle's handwriting.

His expectation of success was framed upon a number of what seemed very favourable circumstances. Neither of the subscribing witnesses were in this part of the country. One, it was known, had gone to England as a refugee and had not since been heard of, and no information could be obtained of the other. Public sentiment, which has always a powerful influence upon juries, was strongly in favor of the claimant. I was a minor, born in a foreign country, and son of a tory who had fled to England at the commencement of the struggle for independence, and most of my connexions had taken the same side in politics. It was thought probable that I might have imbibed the aristocratical notions of the country of my birth, and might be disposed to continue the entail upon the estate, and transmit it tied up and trammeled to my posterity, thereby checking the progress of the country. But whatever my disposition might be, as no title to the soil could be acquired during my minority, which would yet continue for some years longer, the country would be deprived of the benefit of a place of business, for which the mouth of the Cobbosseecontee with its numerous falls was well adapted.

On the other hand the claimant had made it known that if he prevailed, the lands would be at once brought into the market and sold at such low rates as would command immediate purchasers, and a town would immediately spring up to the great advantage of the country around. To overcome these prejudices and convince a jury that the deed produced was a forgery required the strongest evidence, and my father set himself earnestly at work to obtain it. Of the two witnesses to the deed one was presumed to be fictitious, as no evidence could be discovered that such a person had ever lived. The other was Edward Caznean. He had for many years been employed in putting up medicines for country doctors and dealers in Dr. Gardiner's druggist store.

My father could not for some time get any information about him, but at length ascertained that having gone to England as a refugee, he had returned to this country and was living in Charleston, S. C., where he supported himself as a bachelor by practising medicine. My father immediately sent for him. He came and resided in our family for many years. His evidence was direct and positive that the signature to the deed purporting to be his was not genuine, that he had been for a long course of years employed by Dr. Gardiner in superintending the supplies sent by him to Kennebec, and from the direction given to him as to the entries to be made in the books, and also from his conversation, it was apparent that the Doctor never meant to relinquish the property during his lifetime. This testimony was fully confirmed by Mrs. Powell, who had been Dr. Gardiner's wife, and had lived with him till his decease. When Wm. Gardiner became apprized of this testimony he probably lost all confidence in the success of his suit and obtained the commission of lieutenant in John Adams' Oxford Army so called. Upon the disbanding of this army, friendless and poor, he was glad to accept a clerkship in the brewery of Mr. Allen, an Englishman, whose only child, a daughter, he married, and upon the death of her parents acquired from them a handsome property and removed to Richmond on this river. He left a son and two daughters, one the wife of the Rev. Thos. F. Fales of Waltham.

The cause, after being in court about six years, was finally decided by a verdict in my favor. The principal counsel employed by my father was Mr. Sullivan, subsequently Governor of Massachusetts. It had been very expensive, and no costs could be recovered from the administrator of a bankrupt estate. The pendency of this suit deterred my father from doing anything to improve the property. Tho' personally brave, he was morally timid, and feared to prosecute depredators, lest he should increase the prejudices against my title. From the commencement of the revolutionary troubles till I became of age, a period of nearly 30 years, the property was neglected, the timber plundered, and much of the land taken possession of by squatters.

Previous to the American revolution, Dr. Gardiner had made great exertions to settle this township. He had cleared a farm, built a number of houses, a grist mill, fulling mill, saw mills, potash works, and a wharf, and did whatever was necessary for the prosperity of a village in its incipient state. He had given away 50 or 60 lots of from 5 to 10 acres each in the neighborhood of his mills, and had aided the persons to whom he had given them with money to erect their buildings. For these advances he took mortgages on the lots improved, but these people being improvident, most of the lots with their improvements fell back into his hands for the advances he had made, so that, when I came into possession there were only 11 families who had any title to lots occupied, and these lots did not altogether contain 100 acres. But while the township was neglected, lands were taken possession of by squatters, and

I found 86 families settled upon this property without title, and who were in combination with the squatters in the other parts of the country. Gardiner has greater natural advantages than any place on the Kennebec River above Bath, but from the circumstances just related it had made no progress from the time Dr. Gardiner left it 30 years previously, while Hallowell and Augusta, immediately above, had both become flourishing villages, with good roads to the agricultural townships in the interior.

Such was the state of the country, and such the state of my inheritance, when I, an inexperienced young man, was to undertake its management. For this I was in no way prepared. I had not the slightest knowledge of business, my tastes and pursuits having been altogether social and literary, nor was there any one to whom I could look for guidance. My father came with me to Kennebec when I was to assume the management of this property. He had never been fond of business, and having for a long time been disused to its transaction, he had acquired a great dislike to its pursuit. On a rainy day he would bring out some bundles of papers relating to the estates of which he was executor with a countenance as gloomy as the weather, but upon the first plausible pretence they were replaced in their desk to remain till the next rainy day. He was keenly alive to my success, and would have done any thing to promote it, but distrusting his own judgment, he would not attempt to guide mine. Mr. Charles Vaughan was extremely friendly and kind, and had much experience as a land agent, and my father had confided to him the management of the Hallowell lands in which his family were interested. He would doubtless cheerfully have given me advice had I asked it, but he was so entirely deficient in all method, his papers were kept in so confused a manner, that he could never find at the proper time what was wanted, and as he had never succeeded in any thing he had undertaken, I felt it would be better not to ask advice which it might not be prudent to follow.

I was obliged to Mr. Vaughan for the recommendation of Solomon Adams as a surveyor, who proved to be upright and intelligent. He had my entire confidence, and the settlers became satisfied of his integrity, and, what is rare in this land of independence and republican equality, he was perfectly loyal. He had been a soldier in the revolutionary war, and on his return home, when discharged, his breakfast cost him a month's pay in the depreciated paper currency with which his services had been paid. Mr. Monroe, when President, felt the unavoidable injustice with which the revolutionary soldiers had been treated and recommended that they should receive a suitable compensation, and Congress passed an act giving pensions to those who were in want. The old squire complained to me that while he, who by industry and prudence had acquired some property, received nothing, his neighbour, who had spent all his earnings to degrade himself by liquor, received a pension of $96 per annum. Subsequently, Congress gave pensions to all, whether rich or poor.*

It being impossible to make surveys perfectly accurate in a wilderness without going to more expense than the value of the lands, in reply to his question as to the closeness of the measure he should make, I directed him to make it sufficiently large to hold out when the lots were divided but not to leave sufficient surplus to quarrel about, but as land has become more valuable and its clearance of trees has permitted more correct surveys, there have been many quarrels and some law suits for the surplus.

Adams was deficient in education. I therefore employed my evenings in plotting down his surveys and casting the contents of the lots. A good deal had to be accomplished

*Note of R. H. G. 2nd.

One of the early labours entrusted to Squire Adams was to ascertain the true line between Gardiner and Hallowell. The latter town claimed from Gardiner a strip of land some rods in width and 6 miles long. Squire Adams was directed to find the true line. He made inquiries of an old woman then living upon the river bank at the foot of the hill as you enter the village at Bowman's Point. She told him that her husband had been one of the chainmen when the line was run, and that on returning home he told her the line started from the centre of a small island in front of their house. The island had been washed away but a shoal remained. Squire Adams, starting from this, ran the course W.N.W. 6 miles, and then came upon an old beech tree described in the survey as the corner; with an axe he cut deeply into the tree, and came to the surveyor's mark. The chip cut out and produced in court, showing by its rings the number of years since the line was run, with the Squire's evidence, decided the case in favour of Gardiner.

before these surveys could be commenced. The estate was entailed upon my children according to the right of primogeniture, and in default of my having direct heirs, the property was to pass to my cousin, Sylvester Whipple. This entail would so seriously interfere with the management of the property that my friends in this instance volunteered their advice, which I followed, by at once proceeding to break the entail, and to compensate Sylvester for thus frustrating his expectations. I employed Mr. Wilde to conduct the legal process, who adopted the old English cumbrous mode of fine and recovery, and according to their estimate of what Whipple should receive, I engaged to pay him $1000 per annum for five successive years. Sylvester left college before completing his course in order to enter John Adams' Oxford army, in which he obtained a lieutenant's commission. His disposition was amiable but unsocial, and from what has been said of his parents, he could not have received from them any high moral principles. He had a taste for the beauties of nature and loved to wander about the fields and woods, without any knowledge of botany, but merely to collect the flowers that pleased his eye. His sister was impressed with the belief that a disappointment in an early attachment had caused these unsocial and desultory habits. He turned the notes I had given him into cash, and in connection with a partner opened a store in Hallowell, but his partner was not a man of business, and in the course of a couple of years they had sunk most of the capital with which they commenced, and the partnership was dissolved, and the store closed. Whipple did not undertake any other business but continued for two or three years the same homeless, lonely being that he had ever been, and then died.

CHAPTER 8

TROUBLE WITH SQUATTERS

Having relieved the property from the encumbrance of the entail, the next important object was, if possible, to come to some amicable arrangement with the squatters who had possession of so large a portion of the township.

I have before stated how important the squatters considered it, that the link at Gardiner connecting those on the east of the Kennebec should not be broken, and to prevent the Gardiner squatters from making any agreement with the proprietor, they circulated all imaginary stories against my title, some of them palpably absurd, but as the falsehood of one was exposed, another was ready to supply its place. The gist of them all was that my title was good for nothing, and that I should be speedily obliged to abandon the whole estate.

Finding it impossible to make any agreement with them individually, I issued a circular addressed to each squatter on my lands, requesting him to meet me at 2 P. M. on the 11th of August at a room that I had engaged for the occasion, in order to ascertain whether we could not come to some arrangement respecting the lands they occupied and of which I claimed to be the owner.

The meeting was generally attended, but with the squatters came a number of their squatter friends and connections from Litchfield, for the purpose of preventing, if possible, any agreement being made. The room was crowded, and I soon found, from the interference of the men from Litchfield, that it would be impossible for me to effect any thing so long as they remained, but they were not disposed to leave at my request. I then went up to the principal spokesman and took him by the arm and led him out of the room. He was a man over 6 feet high, who could easily have taken me by one hand and thrown me out of the room, but as he was conscious that he had no right there he made no resistance, and the other Litchfield people followed him. As soon as I found myself alone with my squatters, in order to prevent further interruption I locked the door and put the key in my pocket, nor was it again opened till I had come to an agreement with every man in the room, and till I had drawn up a contract which was signed by all present, when I called in persons to witness it.

By this agreement, I was to fix the price of the land to recent settlers at what lands similarly situated were supposed to be worth, and a reduction in price was to be made to the older settlers, in proportion to the time their lots had been improved. They were to receive good warrantee deeds. The payments to be in four equal annual installments, with interest, secured by a mortgage of the premises. If, however, they did not choose to purchase, then their betterments were to be valued by referees mutually chosen, and they were to receive one half the valuation as soon as the award was made, to remain on the land 20 months, taking off two crops, and to receive the other half of the valuation when they left the premises. These terms were more favorable to the settlers than were given by any of the betterment laws passed some years subsequently. The price I fixed was $5 per acre for the lands longest settled, rising to $6.20 for the most recent. Forty nine of my settlers took deeds of the land on which they lived on the terms I offered, and 37 received payment for their betterments. In determining the value of these betterments the referees, instead of taking into consideration the comparative value of the lands in the state they then were, with the value if they had remained in a state of nature, estimated the value of the labour which the settler had bestowed, without considering whether that labour had benefited the land or not, nor did they make any deduction for what he had received for timber sold from the land. In many cases the settlers had merely cut down the trees and burnt them, taking off a single crop, and by allowing the logs to lie on the ground and sprouts and bushes to grow up, had made the land much more difficult to clean and of course of less value, than if no labour had been expended upon it. In general the lands were in a wretched state, the fences only of brush, with log hovels for houses, and log barns. For these betterments, if such they could be called, I paid $5334, the highest sum awarded to any one being $400 and the lowest $16.

Viewed in one light this money was sunk without any equivalent being obtained for it, the lands on the whole being made worse by what had been done to them, but in a higher point of view, the money had been well expended; it had purchased what money can rarely procure, peace, harmony, and good-will.

Confidence was at once established between the settlers and proprietor, early and rapid sales of land followed at enhanced prices, so that notwithstanding the removal from town of the families who sold their betterments, the number of inhabitants in the township doubled between 1803 and 1810. Even in a pecuniary point of view, it is not improbable that the enforcement of my rights by process of law against persons from whom nothing could be recovered would have cost as much money. It would have produced scenes of violence that would have deterred peaceful people from coming into the place. Most of those whose betterments I had purchased left the town at the expiration of the twenty months, many of them to become squatters elsewhere, and most of those who remained in a few years sold their places and moved away. But one of the original, and many of the descendants of others, are still inhabitants of the town and have become valuable citizens.

One only of the squatters, James Dunlap, refused to accede to any terms of settlement. He was the oldest among them, was very ignorant, and acted under the advice of his relatives in Litchfield. He had upon first coming into the township run a line round several hundred acres, which he claimed as his possession, and from it had sold nominal rights to other settlers, from whom he had received much more money than I asked him for the fee of the lot on which he resided. Having settled amicably with every other settler, and being on friendly terms with them, I felt extremely reluctant to be obliged to resort to harsh measures with the remaining one, who was, I knew, acting under the influence of designing men, who were using him for their own purposes. I tried personally to induce him to settle by tempting proposals, offering to sell to him at the very lowest price, and two years without interest, to give him as long a credit as he should desire, or if he preferred to leave, I would give him double what his betterments should be apprised at. I employed persons who I thought might influence him to persuade him to come to terms, but all in vain.

The more I seemed desirous to settle with him, and the more advantageous the terms I offered, the more resolute he become in resisting, being persuaded by his Litchfield connexions that I would not dare to attempt to remove him forcibly, and that they would prevent my doing it if I would, and that these offers were sufficient evidence that I was afraid to attempt it.

I had his betterments appraised by the same referees who had appraised others, and taking a witness with me went out to tender him the amount. But the moment he saw me coming with my bag of dollars in my hand, and before I could explain myself, he fled into the woods and hid himself till I was gone.

I had then no alternative but to eject him by process of law. When I obtained my judgment, he resisted the service of the execution. This I expected, and I then procured a warrant against him for resisting an officer in the course of his duty. I was informed that he had made preparations to prevent an arrest under the warrant, that he kept a large kettle of water hot night and day, and stones collected in his loft to defend himself, and that by blowing a horn, a large number of his Litchfield friends, who lived across the stream in sight of his house, would come to his rescue. It was therefore necessary to take him by surprise. For this purpose I hired a number of resolute men to accompany the sheriff, with directions to start in the night so as to reach Dunlap's house by break of day before he or his friends were likely to be up. They succeeded in reaching the house without giving any alarm, forced the door, took Dunlap and his son out of bed, and hurried them off to jail. I had directed them to tear down the hovel in which he lived, and went out myself an hour or two afterwards to see that this was done, and that their little stock of furniture was taken care of. I found a large collection of people round the ruins, and among them several of the Litchfield squatters, but they offered me neither violence or insult. Dunlap and his son not having been able to obtain bail, remained in jail till the next session of the court.

The grand jury found a true bill against them, and as the facts could not be disputed, they were persuaded to plead guilty.

Considering them as the mere tools of others, I requested the Attorney General to state their case to the court and suggest a very slight punishment, which I think was only a few days imprisonment in the common jail. To prove that I had no vindictive feelings towards this obstinate man, I told him that notwithstanding all that had occurred, I should pay him what his betterments had been apprised at, which was $200., but that I should deduct from it the costs and expenses I had been obliged to pay in getting him off, and I then paid him the balance.

This act of determination in enforcing my rights, at the same time that I did not allow the vexatious misconduct of a misguided man to prevent my allowing claims that he had justly forfeited, had a very happy effect in all future intercourse with these people. One other only gave me any trouble.

Charles McCausland had his betterments appraised and had received half the amount and given an obligation to quit at the expiration of the 20 months. But soon after receiving his first payment he came to me in great distress, saying that an execution had been recovered against him and that he was about to be taken to jail, which I could prevent if I would advance him the other half of the appraisal to which he would be entitled when he left the premises, and for which he should be most grateful. This I did, but at the end of the 20 months he absolutely refused to go, and I was subjected to the necessity and expense of removing him by process of law. Such a person could excite no sympathy. One of his sons worked on my farm and is now a respectable farmer in West Gardiner, and a daughter of his, after living with us many years, was married in our parlour to a man who had been my coachman and had now become presiding elder in the Methodist connexion. They were highly respectable. Their daughter is the wife of the principal of the Readfield Institution.

The suspicions of the settlers had not been altogether allayed, and they objected to my deeds because, adopting the forms there in use, there was no warranty against my heirs. It was in vain I told them that whatever property I had was holden to make good my warranty, and that I had no power beyond that to bind my heirs. I told them at length that the deeds, which my lawyers considered sufficient to convey a good title, had been prepared at my expense, but they might have others prepared as they wished, and I would sign them. I had also much trouble in getting the wife's signature to their mortgages, at that time deemed necessary, but since decided otherwise, when the deed and mortgage bear even date. I was generally obliged to give the wife a new gown or some other present to obtain the signature.

The difficulties between the Proprietors* and settlers continued for eight years after my agreement with those on my lands, during which time all attempts for the survey of the lands of squatters or the service of writs of ejectment against them were successfully resisted. Officers were threatened and in some cases the barns of obnoxious persons were burnt, but no act of personal violence had been committed till 1809, when Paul Chadwick, himself a squatter, was induced secretly to assist in the survey of the land of one of his neighbors. He was therefore deemed to be a traitor who had been bribed to betray his friends and neighbours, and a large party was formed to inflict upon him the penalty which they deemed his treachery to deserve, and he was shot with the surveyor's chain in his hands.

Ten of the party were arrested and safely lodged in jail. One was used as state's evidence, the others were tried for murder. The squatters immediately formed themselves into an armed band for the rescue of their friends. To protect the jail, several companies of militia were called out by the

*Proprietors of the Kennebec Purchase.

state. From the known sympathies of the people, it was doubtful if they would have resisted the attempt to rescue had it been made, but their loyalty was not put to the test. Both parties continued under arms for four weeks, till the termination of the trial. A large number of jury men had been drawn, but all the most respectable were excused as having expressed an opinion in the case, or were preemptorily challenged by the counsel for the prisoners, so the trial was before a packed jury of squatters or the associates of squatters. The trial lasted a fortnight. There was the strongest circumstantial evidence against the prisoners, and the direct testimony of one who had turned state's evidence. Yet they were all acquitted. It was argued that it was not right that nine men should be hung for murder of one. But even if only the most guilty had been tried, it is hardly probable that the verdict would have been different.*

The effect of the trial was upon the whole beneficial, although the verdict was directly contrary to the evidence. The majesty of the law had been supported by the trial of the culprits. The squatters, tho' they had escaped the punishment of their evil deeds, had been subjected to a heavy expense, and, tho' they had prevented the proprietors from enforcing their claims, they were no nearer obtaining a title to their lands than they had been before.

The proprietors also found that the trial had given them no relief. Both parties were therefore more disposed to compromise and to acquiesce in the betterment law passed two years afterwards, which, though it prevented the settlers from being ousted without compensation, was not so favorable to them as the settlers had obtained by their agreement with me. Several of the parties engaged in the murder of Chadwick became peaceable and respectable citizens.

They had murdered Chadwick not for assisting the proprietors, for they offered no violence to the surveyor whom

*Note of R. H. G. 2nd.

This most important trial, so deeply interesting to the whole country, was accurately reported by Mr. Merrick who possessed the accomplishment, so very rare in those days, of writing shorthand. It was published in pamphlet form and was in the Library at Oaklands.

he was assisting, or to the other chainmen, but for the betrayal of his friends. Nor did the act produce lasting animosity between the connections of the two parties, for friendly intercourse and marriage took place between them.

A few months previous to this act of violence, the Plymouth Company discovered that they had by mistake granted to the heirs of James Bowdoin a tract of land in Litchfield between the Cobbossee Contee River and Winthrop Road, which they had previously granted to my grandfather Gardiner, and which he had bequeathed to me and as some of the lands had passed into the hands of third persons they became desirous of obtaining my release, and offered me a tract in Malta among the squatters. As the land was of superior quality I did not hesitate to accept the offer, having no fears that I should thereby excite their hostility against myself.

If they had wished to injure me I was at their mercy, having no man living with me, only a cowardly boy, and, excepting the small farmhouse, there was no house on the same side of the river within a half a mile. My confidence was not misplaced.

The date of my grant was while Chadwick's murderers were in jail waiting to be tried, but within a few weeks afterwards I had settled, on terms perfectly satisfactory, with all the squatters, including two who had just been acquitted.

I cannot but attribute this to the favorable impression made upon them by the course I had adopted towards the squatters in Gardiner.

CHAPTER 9

NEIGHBORS IN 1803

Before proceeding further, it may not be amiss to take a cursory survey of the country and of the state of the society shortly previous to this time (1803).

I have mentioned that the place had not advanced since my grandfather relinquished its superintendence thirty years before. It had, in fact, retrograded actually as well as comparatively, for some of the works and mills which he had established had fallen into decay, without there being any new ones to replace them. There were four or five small shops, where little was kept beyond a few groceries, and we were obliged to go to Hallowell for the commonest hardware or any piece goods beyond cotton sheetings. The mail came to us twice a week in 3½ days from Boston, once by way of New Gloucester and once by way of Wiscasset, which was then the second town in importance in the state. It was brought on horseback, and all the correspondence of the country for three days, with its newspapers and pamphlets, were brought in a pair of saddlebags which did not add much to the burden of the horse.

There were good roads from Hallowell and Augusta to the towns in the interior, but the only road in this town for wheels was from the upper mills to the river, the distance of about a mile. Social visiting was made by water, and the almanac was often consulted to ascertain when the tide would suit for a visit to Hallowell.

The nucleus of future towns and villages existed at several points on the Kennebec River between Bath and Winslow, a distance of 48 miles, but at no place were there collected more than 3 or 4 families of much cultivation. Social ties were necessarily extended and embraced all within the above limits. Providing the comforts of life for their families occupied everyone during the short summer season, but with winter came comparative leisure. The frozen river and snow covered roads afforded facilities for travelling which were wanting at all other seasons. Winter therefore was devoted to social recreation, and, as distances were too great to allow frequent visitings, as many members of a family as could conveniently leave home at the same time set out upon an excursion for a week or two, spending several days at the house of each acquaintance in succession, and at the conclusion of a visit, the host frequently joined in going to the next place.

It is true that the houses were neither large nor convenient, but hospitality had no limits. Those for whom there were no beds slept on the floor or on the haymow. Furnaces were unknown, but wood was abundant, and large fires kept the house warm. The time was spent in social amusements, of which dancing and cards were the principal. The long continued absences from social intercourse gave zest to these gatherings. Inconveniences were disregarded. All were disposed to be gay and to make the best of everything, and if there was not much refinement, there was much more enjoyment than in the showy parties in city life. These winter visiting parties had nearly passed away when I first came here, but there was occasional summer frolicking in somewhat the same style.

During my first summer here, I was invited to join a party from Hallowell to Winslow. One of the long flat bottom boats built to go over the rapids below that place was engaged and fitted up with awnings and benches. Ample refreshments and a band of music were provided. But on the day fixed there was a most violent northerly wind which continued till the third day, and then, tho' the wind was not exhausted, the patience of the party was, and they determined to disregard all obstacles and set off. I hoped to escape, but a horse and wagon were sent after me, and I was taken to meet the boat, which had got as far as Augusta bridge, where I joined and found about 30 young men and as many young ladies on board, who gave me a cordial greeting. These boats carry a large square sail, and, as they draw but little water, they are carried along very swiftly when they are light and the wind is fair. When it is not, the men get them along by rowing or, where the water is shallow, by poling, but our party formed a heavy load for the boat, and we had not proceeded more than a couple of miles above the bridge, before the boatmen gave out, saying that they could not possibly propel the boat against so strong a wind and current. There was too much spirit in the party to yield to such difficulties. A consultation was held, at which it was decided to divide the gentlemen into two parties, one to go into the water and drag the boat by means of a long rope over their shoulders, while the other party should dance with the ladies, and change every half hour.

In this way we proceeded and reached our destination, Thomas's Tavern at Fort Halifax, now Winslow, about midnight. The fire was of course out, and the family gone to bed. We roused them and after a time got ourselves dry and warm, and ate a hearty supper.

As there were beds for but a small portion of the party, it was arranged that the gentlemen should sleep on the haymow, and the ladies on cloaks on the floor. We had not lain long enough on the hay to get fairly asleep, before a message came from the ladies that they could not sleep, and therefore had determined to keep up the frolick by dancing till morning. Tired as we were, we were obliged to obey the summons, and danced till the hour came for an early breakfast. We then found that the wind had changed and blew as violently from the south as it had the day before from the north. The current, however, was strong in our favor, and with its aid the boatmen got us back by sunset, thoroughly tired out, and having paid for our frolic rather dearly.

Hallowell and Augusta had by this time increased so much as to have a social circle of their own, and they were sufficiently near each other for convenient visiting. In both places a number of professional gentlemen had established themselves, and Augusta, recently set off from Hallowell, had become the shire town of the new county of Kennebec.

There Col. Howard kept up the simple hospitality of a

previous period. It was said that the fire never went out on his hearths.

He lived in the old fort, built as a protection against the Indians, and of which his father had been the first commandant. Here he welcomed all, of whatever degree, who came to visit him. Nor were the natives of the forest, who were so long looked upon with terror and were still regarded by most of the community in the light of noxious wild beasts to be exterminated, exempted from his kindness. They came when they chose and remained as long as they pleased, sleeping on the kitchen hearth, being sure of having all their wants supplied by one who did not forget that the Indian had been once sole proprietor of the soil.

Hallowell was at this time much the largest town on the Kennebec, with a cultivated society very rarely found in places with so small a population. Its greatest distinction, however, arose from the Vaughan connection.

Mr. Samuel Vaughan, who had married my aunt, was a republican in principle and a great admirer of everything American. He had embraced all the doctrines of the Utilitarian school and had instilled them into his children so thoroughly as to make them the governing principles of their lives. Previous to the Revolution he had become well acquainted with all the distinguished persons residing in London as agents of the various American colonies, who were frequent guests at his house, particularly with Dr. Franklin, the great propounder of the utilitarian doctrine, for whom the whole family felt a profound veneration. Immediately after the peace of 1783, with a large portion of his family, Mr. Vaughan came to America to observe the progress of the country he so much admired. His oldest son, Benjamin, being then a member of Parliament, he left in England, as he did his daughter Darby and his son William, whom he had taken into partnership. The others accompanied him here. Samuel, the youngest son, subsequently went to Jamaica as agent of the family estates.

Another family at Hallowell with which we were on friendly terms was Judge Wilde's. He was subsequently one of the judges of the supreme court of Massachusetts, and on the separation of the state in 1820 removed to Newburyport in order to retain his office. He was a man of inflexible integrity and was equally distinguished for his ability as an advocate and for the urbanity of his manners, and like most gentlemen of the legal profession had great power of expressing his thoughts, and was very agreeable in society.

He possessed great firmness, and his imperturbable temper was sorely tried by the misconduct of his children, but tho' he suffered very acutely on their account, yet his most intimate friend Judge Parker, who had restrained him by his advice when in early life there was danger of his yielding to the seductions of pleasure, told me that he never knew him but once show emotion on the subject. When out on the circuit we met frequently, for he was social and agreeable, and as he was counsel for the Hallowell estate, which had become very complicated by the interminable trust deeds of the Vaughan family, we met frequently at the dinner table, professedly upon business, which, however, occupied but a small portion of our time.

My classmate Bond studied law with Wilde and became his partner, and tho' a man of principle and good abilities, he had not the social qualities of the judge.

There were 3 or 4 other families at Hallowell with whom we exchanged a rare visit. Augusta at this time was a smaller place than Hallowell, and small as the society was, it was split up into factions by 3 or 4 unquiet spirits who held no intercourse with each other, and the gentlemen were fond of high play.

After the separation of Maine some of the most troublesome spirits moved away, and the whole community were induced to forget their petty feuds by the absorbing object of obtaining the seat of government, by which every one felt that his fortune and individual consequence would be promoted.

Our acquaintance was confined to the families of Benjamin Whitwell, Judge Fuller, and Major Howard, the brother of Mrs. Gardiner, wife of my cousin Rev. Dr. Gardiner.

My classmate, Enoch Tappan, after having lived several years in the middle states, removed to Augusta. His abilities were moderate, and he had obtained no distinction at college, but he acquired considerable knowledge of modern literature, and we found him quite agreeable when he came to dine with us, but he joined his brother's church, a change came over him, and he gave up all social intercourse. He died a bachelor in 1847.

The society of this place was much more limited than in the two towns above. General Dearborn, who had accompanied Arnold in his unfortunate expedition to Quebec, upon retiring from the army had been induced by Mr. Bowdoin to take charge of, and be concerned with him in, lumbering operations on timber lands he owned at Monmouth.

He built mills at the outlet of South Pond in that town, and the lumber was taken, partly by rafting and partly by carting, to this place, where Dearborn fixed his residence for the convenience of disposing of it.

He built a convenient cottage on a lot which my uncle, having no power to give deeds, leased to him at a nominal rent for 99 years, and of which I confirmed the title upon coming of age. Gen. Dearborn possessed a quick and sound judgment, to which he united great energy and promptness in action. These qualities admirably adapted him for a pioneer in a new settlement. He assumed an authority which he exercised somewhat arbitrarily but which was very useful where the restraints of law were feeble and could only be enforced with difficulty. In exercising the duties of a magistrate he resorted to primitive usage and rarely allowed a culprit, when convicted, to leave his presence without receiving the reward of his evil deeds.

He was regarded by the masses with great reverence almost amounting to awe. Upon the organization of the general government he expected to be appointed marshall of the district of Maine, to which he considered himself entitled by his revolutionary services, but the office was given to Isaac Parker, a young lawyer from Boston settled at Castine, and who afterwards became Chief Justice of Massachusetts. Dearborn, soured by this disappointment, became an opponent of Washington's administration and was elected to Congress by the Democratic party. He there became acquainted with Jefferson, who, upon obtaining the presidency in 1801, made Dearborn secretary of war. He immediately removed to Washington with his family, and notwithstanding his violent denunciations against the elder Adams for his nepotism made ample provision from the public crib for his own numerous connexions.

He was subsequently collector of the port of Boston, and in the year 1814 commanded the forces of the U. S. on the Canadian frontier and afterwards [was] minister to Spain, situations to which his talents were not equal. While he resided here, he acted as agent for my father. His disposition was very social, and we were always on the most friendly terms. His own descendants now reside in Portland and those of his second wife still continue in this place.

Our next most prominent resident was Barzillai Gannet. He was a graduate of Harvard in 1785 and had been a licentiate for the congregational ministry. What induced him to fix upon this place as a residence I do not know, but when the County of Lincoln was divided in 1797, and the County of Kennebec established, he obtained the office of clerk of the sessions, and, when the town was incorporated in 1803 he became the first postmaster. By his superior education and his correct and demure deportment he acquired the respect of the community and married a most amiable woman, a Miss Farley, from a highly respectable family. The extreme neatness and clearness of his handwriting added to his reputation. He was annually elected to the principal municipal offices in town and was a general referee in all disputes among his neighbors. He was also a communicant of the church, when its whole numbers might be counted on the fingers, and for many years was its first warden. He was a kind and indulgent husband and excellent father, taking great pains to instill good principles into his children, whom he regularly instructed in the catechism. But with all these good qualities he was not true at heart. He seems to have adopted a species of casuistry by which a certain amount of sin might be atoned for by an extra amount of piety, as if God kept an account current with his creatures, and if the balance was on the side of piety, all would be right at last. Such casuistry tho' rarely avowed is frequently acted upon.

There were a few other families here with whom we occasionally exchanged visits. The Gays, Bradstreets, Parkers, Jewetts and Byrams. Some of them have entirely disappeared from the stage of life, as have the older members of all of them, while the descendants of some still continue here.

CHAPTER 10

TRAVELS IN THE SOUTH

My first season's work here [1803] was continued beyond the middle of December, when the season demanded repose from out door labour, and I returned to my father's in Boston. I had gone thru' a season of very severe labour, both mentally and bodily, and my health had improved under it. Still my friends considered it would be prudent to spend the ensuing winter in the milder climate of the south.

I engaged my friend Gorham to go with me, and we took the best letters of introduction to the first people in the principal cities on our route, making our journey leisurely, staying as long at each place as we might find it agreeable.

In looking back to the customs of society which I witnessed at the various cities that we visited, as well as of those of Boston, I see that very great and beneficial changes have taken place in the use of wine and ardent spirits, and also in the outward respect paid to religion. Wine then formed the chief topic of discussion at dinner parties, and gentlemen continued the drinking till a late hour in the evening, when they finished with a dram under the name of some fashionable liquor. Stimulants were always kept on the side board and offered to morning visitors. In Boston it was wine and some kind of bitters, in Baltimore apple toddy, and farther south, mint juleps. The Boston merchants, before leaving change, took their glass of hot punch at the Bunch of Grapes Tavern, and when gentlemen at evening parties talked thick or looked silly, the ladies would merely remark that they had been dining out, which was considered a sufficient excuse. Guests were watched that their glass was duly emptied before the bottle came around to them again. We dined with Mr. Hammond, a wealthy merchant of New York, with a party of some 15 or 16.

After the cloth was removed and the bottle had passed once around, Mr. Hammond asked what was the duty of the guests when the host opened for them a bottle of very choice wine. Someone replied, 'to see the bottom of it'. He then told the servant to bring up a bishop, when a gallon bottle was produced. 'This,' said he, 'gentlemen, is very fine old wine, the best I have, and as I open it for you, I expect you will finish it.' As a young man not accustomed to using much wine, and yet unwilling to appear uncivil to my host, I disposed of as much as I could among the fruit parings in my plate, and then drank enough to give me a head ache.

There is doubtless still hard drinking at the convivial parties of young men, but I do not believe a counterpart to Mr. Hammond's dinner could be found any where at the present day in any respectable family. A happy change has occurred in the use of wine and ardent spirits, which the teetotalers claim to have produced. Without questioning any good they may have done, it is certain that the change was gradually taking place, long before temperance societies were thought of. Man is not to be made virtuous by placing him where he has not the power to commit sin, but by giving him the ability to resist its allurements.

An equally favorable change has taken place with respect to the observance of religion. The human mind is constantly vibrating from one extreme to the other and rarely continues long in the *juste milieu.* The rigid Puritan discipline of the first half of the seventeenth century was succeeded by the licentiousness of the latter half.

The first half of the 18th saw the rise and expansion of methodism, whose beneficial effect was not confined within the limits of its own sect, but produced a gradual reformation in the other denominations of Christians. At the close of that century, French philosophy had spread its baneful influence throughout the world, banishing the very name of Christianity from the country of its birth, and very many of the educated people in other countries considered religion as a useful means of keeping the masses in order than as a principle of action for themselves.

We found at Philadelphia that, the cares of business being laid aside on Sunday, that day was selected for large dinner parties. Mr. Jefferson, during his long residence in France, had imbibed the deistical as well as the speculative opinions of the French philosophers, and, as president of the United States, gave the tone to society at the Capital. He and his cabinet showed ostentatiously that they considered religion as belonging to a bye gone age, from the trammels of which they were happily released by the advancing knowledge of the 19th century. In Alexandria, in the church where Washington had been accustomed to worship, on a fine day we did not meet a dozen worshippers, and in Richmond, the capital of the state, the old church of St. John's was dilapidated and shut up, and the only other place of worship was a barn looking building, used by the Methodists. The Capitol was occupied on alternate Sundays by an Episcopal or Presbyterian minister from the country.

That Mr. Jefferson did not believe in revelation is now fully established, and yet he would frequently in conversation seem to agree with those who acknowledged its truths. Three gentlemen who had spent at different times some days at Monticello after Mr. Jefferson's retirement from office, related to me conversations that they had had with him upon the subject of religion. To the first, an Unitarian, he observed that unitarianism was the only religion that a sensible man could embrace; to the second, who was a Churchman, that episcopalianism was the only religion for a gentleman; and to the third, whom he deemed a free thinker, that they had put down episcopalianism and the other isms would soon follow. The following anecdote I had from the Rev. Dr. Keith, professor at the Alexandria Seminary, who spoke of it from his own knowledge, and who, I believe, was at one time rector of the church at Charlotteville, and which statement was afterwards confirmed to me by Rev. Dr. Andrews, one of the most distinguished clergymen in Virginia.

He said that on one occasion, when the Episcopal convention met at Charlotteville, Mr. Jefferson came into church when the litany was reading, walked up the broad aisle, unscrewed his cane which made a travelling seat, on which he sat, and, taking a prayer book out of his pocket, made the responses in a very audible voice. At the close of the services, he went up to the clergyman of the place and observed that these conventions, which brought together so many clergy, a large portion of whom he was obliged to entertain, must be very burdensome to persons with their limited income, that he was desirous of contributing his mite towards easing the burden, and that he wished others would do the same, and, taking out his pocket book, handed him a ten dollar bank note, observing at the same time that he had always had a great respect for the Episcopal church, which was the only church for a gentleman.

The Episcopal church in Virginia had been largely endowed with lands by the British government previous to the American Revolution. After the war of independence and principally thro' the influence of Mr. Jefferson, these lands were confiscated by the states and made, I think, an endowment for schools.

A suit was commenced in the state courts to test the constitutionality of the act, and the opinion of a majority of the court was against it, but the Chief Justice, who was ill at the time, died before he could draw up that opinion. Thro' Mr. Jefferson's influence a successor was appointed, hostile to the church, and when the cause was again tried, the validity of the act was sustained. The churches in Alexandria, being in the District of Columbia, were enabled to sue for their lands in the courts of the United States, which declared the law unconstitutional, and their property was restored. Soon after this I was in company with Bishop Madison of Virginia, and asked him if this decision would not induce them to devise some means by which an action could be brought in the U. S. courts for the recovery of the very numerous glebes lying throughout the state. He replied 'No', and then expressed the opinion that a well endowed church independent of its worshippers was rarely in as flourishing a condition as one that depended principally upon the people for its support, an opinion which my own observations made me believe to be correct.

Mr. Jefferson was the first president that undertook to conduct the government on strictly party principles, and I myself experienced the extent to which party prejudices could carry him in social life. When I proposed making my journey to the south, Mr. Benjamin Vaughan offered me a letter of introduction to the President, which I, of course, accepted, observing that Mr. Jefferson had been very intimate in his family when in England, and that he had been able to show him many attentions. Immediately upon my arrival at Washington, I called upon Dr. Eustis, a representative in Congress from Massachusetts, and who was on very intimate terms with my father. He was a leading democrat, and subsequently secretary of war and governor of Massachusetts. He proposed to introduce me to the President, and when I told him that I had a letter of introduction from Mr. Vaughan, he replied, 'So much the better'. We called, and Dr. Eustis introduced me as the son of an old and very particular friend. Mr. Jefferson was dressed in an old blue coat and corduroy breeches with woolen stockings that had been footed with yarn of a different color, and with a dirty and faded scarlet waistcoat. When he first came into the room, I took him for a servant and felt surprised that the President should allow one to remain in his house so shabbily dressed. But this was affectation, in imitation of the French sans culottes. Mr. Jefferson could dress well and knew how to behave as a polished gentleman, but he affected ultra democratic notions, rode on horseback to the capitol without a servant, and fastened his horse to a post.

We conversed very pleasantly for half an hour with the President, and as we came away, Dr. Eustis observed to me that, 'tomorrow you will receive an invitation to dine with the President'. I saw the Dr. every day, and every day he made the same inquiry, if I had received my invitation, and when I every day gave the same negative answer, he expressed great surprise, saying that he had never before introduced a person to the President as he had me without its being immediately followed by an invitation to dine, and seemed to take the omission in my case as a slight to himself.

I told the Doctor that I thought I could explain the mystery. Mr. Vaughan's letter was given to me open, as is usually the case with letters of introduction, and after saying in the letter all the civil things that I could desire, Mr. Vaughan added that I was a Federalist, which was considered by Mr. Jefferson as an unpardonable sin.

Mr. Jefferson acquired a popularity and influence which far exceeded what had been obtained by any president excepting Washington, and to which no one has approached but Jackson.

He had succeeded in overthrowing the Federal party, which 3 years before had an overwhelming majority, and he espoused the cause of the masses against those who were distinguished by their wealth, their learning, and their conservative principles.

He was unquestionably a man of talent, but he was visionary, and tho' his name is still associated with that of Washington, and he is quoted in all popular orations as one of the great founders of the republic, his principles of government have been gradually abandoned. He was opposed to the funded system, to foreign commerce, to a navy, and to large towns. His acquisition of Louisiana, which, by giving us New Orleans and forever settling our difficulties about the free navigation of the Mississippi, was of incalculable benefit to the country, has not been without its disadvantages. The limits of the constitution, as Mr. Jefferson himself acknowledged, were disregarded, and an uncontrollable desire of adding to our immense domain was fostered, which had been producing a taste for war and fillibustering expeditions upon our weaker neighbors.

Mr. Jefferson, by conducting himself in his high office as the head of a party whose interests were paramount to all other considerations, rather than as president of the whole country, introduced the maxim that *to the victor belong the spoils,* making the emoluments of office a scramble for needy politicians, and obliged the high minded statesmen of the country who would not pander to the passions of the mob, to retire to private life.

From Washington we passed rapidly to Charleston, S. C.,

only stopping on our way for a couple of days at Richmond. We had numerous letters to the first people in the state, but such was the hospitality of the people that one of them would have given us an introduction to the first people. Society there was aristocratic and exclusive. Merchants were not ranked as gentlemen, and commercial business was in the hands of New England men or foreigners, principally Scotch. The elite of the society were planters, and even lawyers and physicians, tho' they ranked as gentlemen, were ambitious to attain the higher grade of planters as soon as they could acquire the means. Some of the older gentlemen had been educated in Europe and had a polish of manners rarely found in the north.

The young men had neither the cultivation or refinement of their fathers. As they could find little employment consistent with their aristocratic notions, they fell into habits of dissipation and rowdyism. We were invited to their supper parties, and we always left some unable to find their way home till they had slept off their debauch. Others would go round and wrench the knockers and bell pulls from the street doors. The sufferers did not like to have a strict enquiry made for the authors of these practical jokes, lest their own sons should be found amongst the offenders. Young men of more character and energy went into the adjoining states to form plantations on new land.

By the constitution, congress had no power to interdict the slave trade till 1808, but an act was early passed forbidding it after that date. South Carolina permitted it as long as she had the power to do so, which so far as that state is concerned, is an answer to those southern gentlemen who say the institution was forced upon them by the mother country against their strong remonstrances. We went on board two ships just arrived at Charleston with full cargoes, and were surprised to find the vessels clean, not overcrowded, and the negroes looking healthy and not unhappy, but anxious to display themselves to the best advantage in order to be purchased. The slave trade was as openly carried on in Savannah, tho' contrary to law, as in Carolina. A ship with slaves came to anchor at an island below the city, and when the marshal went down to seize her, his boat was cut adrift, and he could neither get away or be received into any house till he had agreed to go back and stop all proceedings against the vessel. The south retort upon the north that, if they bought slaves, those slaves were brought to them by northern people in northern vessels. There is some truth in this, but the sense of the community, as well as the law, was against it at the north, and the traffic was considered very disreputable. So far as I could judge, slaves were treated well by their masters, were not overworked, and had good care taken of them. A gentleman who should treat them otherwise would lose his position in society. But strangers coming into the state, and the poor man whose only slave had to support both himself and master, had no public sentiment of their equals to restrain their avarice. Hard indeed the fate of the slave who should fall into the hands of such masters.

The character of slavery has not changed during the half century that has elapsed since my youthful journey, but as the denunciations of the abolitionists have become more violent against the institution, the southern laws have become more stringent to keep their slaves in ignorance. Fifty years since, the most enlightened statesmen of the south felt the blighting influence of slavery, but the rapid rise in the price of cotton and the enormous profits which have since been made by its cultivation, have blinded them to its evils, and they now contend for it as a great benefit to the country and a blessing to the slave himself.

It is impossible to speak too highly of the kind and friendly attentions shown to us by the Carolina gentlemen. Every thing was done on the plantations to make our visits agreeable. The treatment of their negroes, the culture of rice, which is peculiar, and to us was novel, and all their other agricultural operations were shown and explained in the most friendly manner, and in passing from one plantation to another, unless the way was too plain to be mistaken, guides were sent with us.

Where the population is too scattered to admit of much social intercourse, as in the southern states, hospitality is more necessary, and the exercise of it more agreeable than in the densely populated states of the north. The heartiness of southern hospitality is extremely agreeable to the traveller.

Among the gentlemen with whom we became more particularly acquainted in Carolina were the Pinckneys, Rutledges, Judge Dessessaure, Col. Washington, a nephew of the general, and Col. Shubrick.

Gen. Charles Cotesworth Pinckney united the frankness of the soldier with the polished manners of a gentleman of the old school, and was very highly esteemed and respected throughout the state. He left no son, and in the subsequent times of nullification his daughters embarked so warmly in the delusion as to injure their fortune. Their father was a warm federalist, and I do not believe his strong sense would have been warped by the abstractions of Calhoun. His brother Thomas, with a less commanding position than the general, was very highly esteemed, but from the situation of his family, we saw less of him. John Rutledge was one of the most polished and accomplished gentlemen with whom I was ever acquainted. He was considered a man of talent and statesman and held a high position in the Senate of the United States. He was extremely cordial and friendly. A short time before we were there, he found a letter from Dr. Senter of Rhode Island written from Europe, making an assignation with his wife. His relative, Col. Shubrick, who related the circumstances, told me that Senter, having forfeited the rights of a man of honour, was to be subjected to summary punishment, and he went with Rutledge in pursuit of him. R. shot him while secreted in an outbuilding on his plantation. This was in conformity with the prevailing notions of the community, and no legal notice was taken of it.

It seems such an act, however opposed to our northern ideas, was repeated with slight variations at Washington, when Sickles shot Key.

When we were at Col. Washington's plantation, he showed us their peculiar mode of hunting, adopted doubtless because violent exercise is not adapted to a warm climate. A parcel of negroes make an extensive circuit and drive the game to a pass in the woods where the sportsmen sit concealed, smoking their cigars till the game appears, when they fire rapidly, their guns being reloaded by negroes in waiting, as fast as discharged, and the amount of game taken is generally large.

In order to visit the plantations with more convenience and make a trip to Savannah, we purchased a pair of horses and a chair, which was a settee large enough to hold two persons, set on shafts without springs. We hired a colored servant who rode one of the horses, while the other carried us in the chair. The deep sandy soil does not admit of good roads, and there were few bridges over water courses. By the laws of most of the southern states the slaves on every plantation are required to work repairing the roads the three first days in August. This work consists principally in cutting out fallen trees, and if a tree should fall across the road on the fourth day, it remains till the next August, and travellers make a track round it, unless some spirited individual should cut it out in the meantime. Our visit to Savannah was not very interesting. Society was in a much newer and ruder state than in Charleston. In returning from the south we took a packet from Charleston to Baltimore, and thence by land to Boston. The tour had been very agreeable and made doubly so by having my friend Gorham with me, as our views and tastes assimilated, and my health, the great object of the tour, had been much improved. I got back here early in May, 1804.

CHAPTER 11

THE ANTHOLOGY CLUB

In December, 1804, I went again to Boston to spend the winter at my father's, dining out almost every day and going to some one or two parties every evening, till I became wearied and disgusted with the nothingness of such social intercourse.

During the winter I was invited to join a club which subsequently assumed the name of the Anthology Club.

A periodical magazine had been commenced by my classmate Phineas Adams, which he conducted under the name of 'Phineas per se', the title showing that it was wholly his work. He obtained a respectable number of subscribers, but not enough to pay the expenses and give him any remuneration, and was obliged to give it up. The publisher thought that with other and more numerous writers it might be made popular, and upon the failure of Adams proposed to some of my friends to continue the publication, or establish some other periodical in its place. I accepted an invitation to join in the undertaking, and we thought it better to have no connection with the former publication of Adams, and determined to establish a new work under the name of 'The Monthly Anthology', to consist partly of original poetry and essays and partly of reviews of American publications.

The club consisted of the Rev. Drs. Gardiner, Kirkland, McKean, and Emerson, Rev. Joseph J. Buckminster, Arthur Maynard, Walter and James Savage, Wm. Tudor, Edmund Dana, and William S. Shaw, and was subsequently joined by George Ticknor, Rev. Samuel Thacher, and John Stickney. The club met weekly, at first at each other's houses, but subsequently at a house in Congress Street occupied by an Englishman who was clerk of Trinity Church and who was distinguished by his skill in the culinary art,

REV. JOHN SILVESTER JOHN GARDINER

By Stuart

and who prepared for the club an excellent supper, consisting simply of beefsteak and oysters with wine and cigars. The first business of the evening was the reading of papers prepared for the next number of the Anthology, which were discussed with great freedom, and, with a solitary exception, with perfect good humor. In one instance McKean, the future professor of oratory at Harvard University, was so much offended at some remarks upon the turgid style of one of his pieces, that he left the club, and never after again met with us. After the business of the evening was completed, the conversation became general, but was exclusively upon literary topics. I do not recollect that any of the exciting topics of the day were ever introduced. Parties both in religion and politics were too bitterly opposed to admit of friendly discussions between them. The conversation was general, the members sitting around the table, and not so numerous as to require breaking up into groups. One discussion was remarkable for being continued thro' several evenings, and being subsequently introduced into the pages of the Anthology and was almost wholly between Mr. Buckminster and Dr. Gardiner upon the merits of Gray as a poet. Mr. Buckminster pointing out the beauties of Gray, and citing his favourite passages; the doctor on the other hand travestying the quotations and ridiculing the imagery, but it was all done in perfectly good humour. Dr. Gardiner, as senior member, always took the head of the table and the lead in conversation, and was the Dr. Johnson of the club. I never belonged to a club where the evenings were so invariably agreeable. No one realized how the evening was passing away till some one had the hardihood to look at his watch and to announce that the midnight hour had gone, when we all at once left. Most of the club were quite young men. Drs. Gardiner and Kirkland were more advanced than the rest of us. Neither of them had the seriousness of deportment associated in the minds of most people with the clerical character. They were both fond of society. Gardiner had been educated in England and therefore indulged in such amusements as were then and there permitted, by public opinion, to the clergy. He frequented the theatres and had the actors frequently at his home. He was fond of cards and was a remarkably graceful dancer. Kirkland was educated amongst the descendants of the Puritans, who, tho' they had departed from the strictness of their fathers, did not tolerate their clergy in partaking of what they considered worldly amusements. Gardiner was frank and open, and had such a rooted dislike to everything that appeared like hypocrisy that he would not refrain from what he deemed innocent amusements tho' he might give to others a false and unfavorable opinion of his character.

An instance of this occurred at New York. Dr. Gardiner was assistant minister at Trinity Church, Boston, upon the pittance of $800. per annum and had nearly exhausted the patrimony he had inherited from our grandfather in supporting his family in the style of a hospitable gentleman. He was invited to New York to preach as a candidate for the office of assistant minister in the very rich and liberal corporation of Trinity Church. His services were acceptable, and the desired invitation would have been given had he not dined with the Belvidere Club on Saturdays, which was composed of Englishmen, and who sat over the bottle regularly till the early hours of the Sabbath morning.

Kirkland, on the contrary, took a pride in not committing himself on controverted subjects, particularly upon the dogmas which were then splitting the congregational body into two hostile parties. Journeying with him for some days in a private hired carriage, we had a good deal of very interesting conversation. Upon religious subjects he always spoke in the third person, as if no one knew, or had a right to know, his thoughts upon them.

He related to me the following anecdote of himself. A lady once asked Judge Parsons what were his (Kirkland's) views of the Trinity. The Judge replied that he did not know. The lady then said, 'I thought, Judge, that you were one of his parishioners'. 'So,' he said, 'I am, and have sat under his preaching for a long course of years, but I never at any time heard him allude to the subject of the Trinity.'

Kirkland had a wonderful insight into human nature. As president of the college he knew the character and conduct of every scholar, but partly from indolence and partly from kindliness of disposition, he was unwilling to use that knowledge in the punishment of delinquents. Kirkland was the man of deeper thought, stronger mind, and more general knowledge. Gardiner was the finer classical scholar and had a keener power of satire. He wrote the Epistle to Zenas, which his father found and published without his knowledge. He also wrote the Jacobinia, a very severe and powerful satire upon the leading democrats, who formed a Jacobin club that met weekly to promote their political views. It was published with caricature likenesses of the leading members. It made them ridiculous and excessively angry, but it was only answered with low abuse. Kirkland had much suavity in his manners, Gardiner was rough and cared not whom he offended. He said to me once, 'Well, Robert, I have preached the last Jacobin out of church.' Neither of them possessed what is called unction, but they both had fine powers of conversation and greatly added to the animation and pleasure of the club.

Savage was well informed on most subjects, and his knowledge accurate and always at hand for use. He could say smart and very pointed things, but he had not then that positive and dictatorial manner in which he imitated Dr. Johnson.

Stickney amused us with puns in the learned languages, and our classical acquirements were still sufficiently fresh to enable us to enter into their spirit. Tudor had a graceful and pleasing humor which never wounded the feelings, but always increased the bonhommie of the club.

Dana had a highly cultivated mind and fine powers of conversation, but as the profits of the anthology did not pay for our suppers, he found it inconvenient to meet the expense and, to our very great regret, left the club, for he was too proud to have the club pay for him.

Walter had a fine mind, which was richly stored. After graduating at Harvard and studying law in Boston, he went to London, pursuing his studies at the Temple, and became intimate with the members of that fraternity and with the distinguished legal characters of Great Britain, and, but for his premature death, would doubtless have become a leading member of his profession.

Shaw was uncouth in mind and body, but was indefatigable in his labour for promoting the success of the work in which we were engaged.

As the circulation of the Anthology increased, so the periodicals we received in exchange accumulated, and books, both original and republications of English works, were constantly sent to us to be reviewed. All these required a place of deposit, and we hired a convenient room in Congress Street opposite our supper room, and as there was then no public reading room in Boston, we opened ours to the public by the payment of a moderate fee, the receipts, after paying the expenses of the room, being appropriated to obtaining valuable periodicals that we did not receive in exchange for the Anthology, and thus adding to its attraction.

Our reading room was eminently successful. Not wishing to incur unnecessary expense, and the club having no funds, Walter, Shaw, and myself removed the books ourselves to our new rooms and arranged them on the shelves.

One of our members, having received an account of the Athenaeum recently established at Liverpool, read it to the club. We were all at once impressed with the great advantage there would be in having such an institution in Boston, and we determined at once that it should be established with the same name.

A prospectus was prepared and issued in the form of a circular to those gentlemen whose aid we expected in the undertaking. It was estimated that 150 individuals could be found in Boston who would pay $300 for a share in the institution, giving two tickets of admission in perpetuity, and with the right of temporary transfer, and so accurately was our estimate made, that all the shares excepting 2 or 3 were at once taken.

Before opening the subscription, it was proposed that the members should each make a donation of books, which was readily complied with. My donation was 'The Universal History' in about 70 octavo volumes. We then purchased the house on Tremont Street next the Chapel burying ground, where is now the building belonging to the Historical Society, which was conveniently fitted up for a reading room and library. Shaw entered most heartily into the plan, was made librarian, and, not being troubled with diffidence, became a sturdy beggar for the Athenaeum, applying for donations of books or pamphlets wherever there was the least prospect of obtaining them, and was very successful. His exertions procured for him the soubriquet of Athenaeum Shaw. His very great and disinterested exertions for the institution palliated his eccentricities and gaucheries, and he continued librarian till the unfortunate habit of intemperance made him incapable of attending to the decencies of life and the trustees were obliged to dismiss him.

CHAPTER 12

MARRIAGE

In the course of the winter (1804-5) I became acquainted with your mother*, and I need not tell you, my dear children, that that acquaintance produced an earnest desire of gaining her affections and of inducing her to share with me the joys and sorrows of this chequered life. In reviewing that long distant period I find that my sanguine expectations of happiness from that union have been more than realized. A natural shyness, with an inability to believe that I could be received as a favored lover, made me hesitate to declare myself. There was a lady, Catherine Russell, well acquainted with us both, who, though single herself, made it the chief pleasure of her life to promote matrimonial unions between those of her friends whose tastes and character were adapted to each other. She was some ten or fifteen years older than ourselves, and had acquired much tact in perceiving the first budding of affection between young persons and making herself their confidant. She told me of my regard for your mother before I was well aware of it myself. Under her encouragement I wrote to your mother declaring my affection, and how much happiness would depend upon its reciprocation. My letter was despatched on a Friday afternoon, and Saturday was the day I was accustomed to drive my father to the regular dinner party at Mr. Jeffrey's at Milton. The state of doubt and anxiety in which I found myself was not calculated to fit me for a pleasant dinner party, but I knew not how to excuse myself from going. I vainly endeavoured to stifle the deep emotions that were struggling within my bosom. My agitation and absence of mind were perceptible to every one, and, as we rode together, my father was continually asking me if I was ill, and if not what could be the matter with me. It was a relief upon our return to town to see him go

*Emma Jane Tudor, daughter of Judge William Tudor.

EMMA JANE TUDOR

ROBERT HALLOWELL GARDINER

Miniatures by Malbone

off to his whist club that I might retire to my chamber to commune in private with my own thoughts.

Your mother's reply, which I did not receive till Monday afternoon, neither accepted nor rejected my suit, but in it she gave me permission to visit her. The answer did not meet my hopes, and I felt much dejected and went with it to my friend Catherine.

She put a different interpretation upon the reply, saying no lady ever gave a professed lover permission to visit her without feeling, though it might be unconsciously, an inclination to accept his suit. I took full advantage of the permission granted and spent every evening with your mother, and it was not long before the engagement was publicly announced. Dr. Gardiner joked me on the occasion, saying that I who professed to be indifferent to beauty was going to marry the handsomest girl in town. I should have liked to have shown my children the early correspondence between their parents, but it was destroyed with many family letters and papers, which would have been now of interest, when my office was burnt. My father readily approved the engagement, and your grandfather Tudor was pleased with it.

Your grandmother did not object to it, but it sadly interfered with the romantic schemes which she had formed for her daughters. Mrs. Tudor had been indued with very considerable mental powers, but her early education had been neglected, and her mind had never been subjected to discipline. Her imagination, naturally vivid, had overpowered her other faculties and she was incapable of any chain of reasoning. She lived in an ideal world, amid the splendid airy castles of her own creation. Incapable of following opinions and actions to their natural consequences, the dictates of prudence made little impression upon her. At a subsequent period, when confidence had grown up between us, she was fond of telling me her visionary plans, and when I would attempt to show her how illusory they were, she would interrupt me by saying that she loved illusion and did not want to be undeceived. She was deficient in that invaluable but homely gift of common sense, which in carrying us safely through the complicated scenes of life is of far greater importance than the splendid gifts of talent and genius. She kept her mind always active, which retained its powers till the close of a very protracted life, nor were her literary pursuits relinquished till its close. She was full of benevolence, and those who from defects of character, from misfortune brought upon themselves by their own misconduct, or even from perversity, had forfeited the sympathy of others, were sure to receive kindness from her. Her temper was most forgiving, and she neither resented nor remembered unkind treatment from those who owed her only respect and affection. To the young she always made herself agreeable, and our children became very fond of her. During the American Revolution many French officers were quartered in Boston at a time when aristocratic descent was the only passport to a royal commission. They were consequently, with very few exceptions, men of polished manners, easy address, and accustomed to make themselves agreeable in the fashionable saloons of Paris. They formed a favorable contrast in the eyes of an imaginative young lady wholly ignorant of mankind, with the homely sense and sturdy independence of her own countrymen. Freqent intercourse with them gave her a strong and enduring taste for the society of foreigners, and an ardent desire to visit Europe, the country of so much refinement. This desire increased in intensity as years rolled on, and as her children were growing up, the wish that they should enjoy the advantages to which she attached such exaggerated importance made her constantly devise schemes for its fulfillment. Your mother had shown a taste for painting, she must become a distinguished artist, for which a few years' residence in Italy would be requisite; and Delia, with her love of study and fondness for the acquisition of foreign language, was to make the acquaintance of the learned men in Europe and become equally distinguished in the walks of literature.

That your mother should consent to unite herself to such a prosaic person as myself was a sad shock to these airy visions.

Mrs. Tudor had a great dislike to long courtships, and the Judge, always impatient of any delay in the accomplishment of anything to which he had once assented, joined Mrs. T. in wishing that the marriage should speedily take place, to which the young people were, of course, not averse. I was obliged to make a visit here in May for a few weeks, and it was determined that the marriage should take place soon after my return. We were accordingly married by my cousin, Rev. Dr. Gardiner, at Trinity Church, Boston, the 25th day of June, 1805, at 8 o'clock in the morning. That early hour was fixed to prevent a crowd of idle spectators, as marriages in church were then unusual, but we were both too much absorbed in our own feelings on that important occasion to be conscious whether we were alone present, making our solemn vows before the altar of God, or were in the presence of hundreds of spectators. After the service, the bridal party, consisting, besides ourselves, of my father, the Judge's family, and Dr. Gardiner's, my groomsman, George Sullivan, and the bridesmaid, [name illegible] breakfasted at your grandfather Tudor's and then went to Rockwood to spend the day.

The party, as was to be expected on such an occasion, were all in fine spirits, and the Judge, who was ever as ready to laugh at himself as at others, kept us amused by his humorous description of his experience in farming. He had built large barns, warm poultry houses, and a convenient dairy, but his hay, his chickens, his eggs, and his butter had all to be procured from the market. In the afternoon the party returned to town, leaving the bride and bridegroom to spend the first half of the honeymoon with your grandmother at Rockwood. I then took your mother with a horse and chaise to Kennebec.

CHAPTER 13

BOSTON SOCIETY

In the winter that I spent in Boston I was much in company. Your mother had not much taste for fashionable evening parties, when the company seemed to be collected principally for the purpose of the ladies to criticize each other's dresses, and which were too crowded to admit of rational conversation, and from which the company seemed disposed to retire at the first practical moment. When she occasionally went, I always accompanied her.

I frequently attended the Wednesday Evening Club, originally established by Mr. C. Vaughan and his friends for promoting intercourse between educated people of different pursuits. It consisted of an equal number of merchants and of each of the three learned professions. They assembled from 8 to 8½ P. M., smoked, conversing in groups till 9½, when they collected round the supper table and partook of a simple repast, of which oysters and fruit were the principal ingredients, and separated soon after 11. When strangers were in town who, it was thought, would harmonize with the company, they were always invited. I found the meetings very agreeable. There were other clubs which I also occasionally attended. One of them a scientific club, instituted by Dr. J. C. Warren, in which a paper on some scientific subject was read and afterwards discussed. It met once a fortnight, but the papers read were generally heavy, and the discussions were not kept up with spirit.

Your mother had taken an interest in Mr. B. Vaughan's second daughter Lucy, who to good sense united warm affections, but who, from a natural awkwardness and shyness, was not a favourite in her father's family. Your mother felt that by spending the winter in Boston with us the shyness would be overcome, and when removed from the overshadowing restraint of her elder sister, the finer points of her character would be developed. My father very readily assented to the proposal, but no sooner was the invitation given, than Mrs. V. came instantly down and begged my father to include also her favorite daughter Sally in the invitation. It was not at all agreeable to my father or your mother, both of whom felt Mrs. V's want of delicacy, but my father did not know how to refuse the request, and both sisters went to Boston with us. Mr. Vaughan had taken great pains to cultivate Sally's mind. She was familiar with English literature, painted prettily, and conversed agreeably, and there was an uncongeniality about her, and a repulsiveness in her manner, which prevented her from being an agreeable inmate. The pleasure of your mother's winter was marred, and Lucy, constantly oppressed with her sister's superiority, was not benefited by the visit as was anticipated. Sally had much of the Vaughan benevolence and was fond of doing kind things, but there was a want of decision about her that ever prevented her from perceiving the clear path of duty, and she hesitated as much as to the propriety of wearing a ribbon of a particular colour as on important action. She had spent some time in England with connections who belonged to the evangelical party, and had imbibed from them strict notions of the requirements of religion, but they were not the ruling principles of her life. Her conscientiousness was morbid, and while indulging in what are considered innocent recreations by Christians, excepting those of the more austere sects, she always felt self reproach that she was not acting up to the requirements of Christian calling. It was impossible for me not to be aware, from my early acquaintance with the family, of their wish, and particularly the desire of Mrs. V., that we should be more intimately connected by my marrying Sally, but our characters were too uncongenial for me ever to have thought of it, and the union, if it had been formed, could not have been happy. At the close of my first summer's residence here, I spent the night previous to my departure at Mr. Vaughan's, and the extreme pleasure I felt, and could not but show, at getting away, first satisfied Mrs. V. that my attractions here were not sufficiently strong to give any hope of fulfillment of her wishes. Sally died in Boston a few years since, unmarried, after a few days' illness.

When in Boston I was constantly invited to dinner parties, probably from the reputation of being hospitable at home, and dined out as often as four or five times a week. Large dinners where the company is promiscuous and you can only converse with the person sitting next to you, are seldom agreeable, but those generally attended rarely exceeded a dozen persons, and were composed of gentlemen of cultivated minds; the conversation was general, and, if not profound, was always sensible.

Mr. William Sullivan was remarkable for making his dinners particularly agreeable, assorting his company and not mixing persons whose views and habits did not assimilate. The person I met most frequently at these dinners was Dr. Kirkland, the President of Harvard College. His conversation, though non-committal where theology was the subject, was rich and free on other subjects. He was never dictatorial, and while his conversation was full of thought, he endeavored to bring out the views of others. I frequently met Mr. Webster and Judge Story, when they were not engaged at Washington. Mr. Webster did not frequently take the lead in company, but when drawn out, he was listened to with the greatest attention. Judge Story was the greatest talker I ever knew, but he talked well. When he was a young man at the Essex bar, I have stopped at night at Ipswich on my journey to Boston, purposely to hear him hold forth to the lawyers assembled at the tavern. I once dined in company with Story, when Webster, Otis, and other gentlemen of that standing were at table. Story engrossed the whole conversation for several hours. Wm. H. Prescott, the historian, who sat next to me, whispered, 'It is too bad. I have been trying for this hour to get in a word edgeways and can't succeed.' Story commenced life as an ultra Republican, and was placed on the bench of the Supreme Court of the U. S. for entertaining those views. But the ermine had wonderful power of changing the opinions of those who are clothed with it, and Story became the most conservative judge on the bench. He was fond of society, but though capable of performing an immense amount of work, yet his duties as judge, as law professor at Cambridge, and as author, gave him too full employment to indulge in it. His law books, though they had not the same authority in England as Kent and Wheaton, gave him reputation both at home and abroad, and the copyright was a source of pecuniary benefit both to himself and his heirs. He published reports of his own decisions and those of the full court, and as proof of his wonderful facility of labour, he told me that when the manuscript of one of his volumes was burnt in the printing office, he was able to re-write it from memory in, I think he said, four months, with only the aid of a few loose notes and the assistance of a few notes of the other judges, notwithstanding his other numerous duties. He was very popular at the law school at Cambridge and did much to establish its reputation, but, excessively fond of flattering himself, he was of disservice to many of his pupils by bestowing on them undeserved or exaggerated praise and making them conceited. After the older members of the Supreme Court, who had received their appointment from their talents and high character, had passed away, their places were filled by inferior men appointed from party motives. Story found that his influence on the bench was gone, and he resigned in disgust. His health had failed, and he did not long survive his retirement.

At a select dinner party given to Jeffrey of the Edinburgh Review, afterwards Lord Jeffrey, I dined with Mr. Otis and a few others of the elite of the town. In the course of conversation Jeffrey referred to a passage in the writings of Jeremy Taylor, when Otis asked who Jeremy Taylor was. Jeffrey replied in his rapid sarcastic manner, 'not know who Jeremy Taylor was' repeating the expression rather contemptuously. This was particularly mortifying to Otis, who though without pretensions to literary distinction, considered himself as the most polished corner of the social temple in New England. Otis was a man of considerable talent and would have acquired great distinctions if he had limited himself to one pursuit, but, being ambitious of obtaining celebrity as a lawyer, an orator, and a statesman, of becoming a man of great wealth and a leader in fashionable circles, he failed of acquiring eminence in any. This rebuff he received from Jeffrey was soon noised round the town, and the booksellers, to prevent an occasion for a similar occurrence, immediately put out a reprint of some of the most popular of Taylor's works. Jeffrey had engrossed most of the conversation and had been listened to with great attention, and he very evidently thought that it was a condescension on his part to have dined with a company of Boston gentlemen.

Before my marriage one Saturday I drove my father to Milton to dine with Patrick Jeffrey, uncle to Lord Jeffrey. He had married the sister of the famous Wilkes, a widow with a large fortune, old enough to be his mother, and not an immaculate character. After living together some time very unhappily, they separated, and she returned to England. When they married, she gave up her whole property to him, from which he made her a liberal allowance.

A nephew and brother of Ld. Jeffrey resided with his uncle, who suffered severely from chronic complaints, which kept him confined to the house. Seeing but few visitors, owing to his distance from Boston, the Saturday's dinner party was a source of very great pleasure to him. The party consisted of Joseph Hall, Judge of Probate, a sensible, shrewd man, Joseph Russell, called Quaker Joe for being of a Quaker family, and to distinguish him from another gentleman of the same name. Without a cultivated mind, he had a great fund of humour and a remarkable ready wit which kept the company amused and in good spirits. The rest of the party consisted of three Generals, —one, Jackson, had no claims to distinction, but both Knox and Cobb had been distinguished officers in the Revolutionary War, and were men of decided character.

At the time of Shay's Rebellion attempts were made to prevent the holding of any courts of justice. Cobb, who was a judge of the Court of common pleas, was forbidden by the mob to hold his court at Taunton, but he told them that if he could not hold it as judge, he would as general, and when they found that he was not to be intimidated, no further resistance was made. Cobb was extravagant in his conversation, and being a prominent Federalist, his imprudent speeches were turned into political capital by his Democratic opponents. Riding in the stage with Genl. King, who was then striving to reach the top of the political ladder, he and Cobb got into a warm political discussion, when Cobb jokingly said to King, 'If you get into power I suppose you will hang all of us Federalists, and (with an oath), if we gain the election, we will hang you.' A few days after, an article appeared in the newspaper stating that a distinguished Federalist, high in office, had publicly stated that they meant to put their opponents to death when they should obtain the power. Knox had been secretary of war under Washington, and to him we are indebted for the military academy at West Point. He had been a good officer and was fond of his profession.

The war in Europe and the great victories of Napoleon, who was changing the boundaries of all the continental states and bringing the descendants of the oldest dynasties to sue for peace at his feet, naturally formed the principal topic of conversation everywhere, but particularly among military men. Knox was a warm Federalist, but his enthusiastic admiration of the military genius of Napoleon outweighed his political partialities. He was always eloquent on this, his favorite theme, and won several beaver hats by bets with others of the party on the success of the great captain. Knox had married a granddaughter of Brigadier Waldo, and partly by inheritance and partly by purchase of confiscated property, had become possessed of the largest portion of the Waldo patent, embracing much fine land, many good harbours, excellent mill privileges, and valuable lime quarries.

He here built a splendid house and lived in the style of an English nobleman. He had an open, generous disposition, was fond of society, and extremely hospitable. He engaged in various schemes of business, all superintended by paid agents, and all losing concerns. He died from attempting to swallow a chicken bone which stuck in his throat. If he had survived a few months longer, his proud spirit would have been obliged to give up his splendid establishment and acknowledge himself a bankrupt.

Lady dinner parties were not frequent. Young people seldom went to them. They were stiff and disagreeable. The gentleman were always expected to say smart things to the ladies, who retired to the drawing room immediately after the bottle had been passed once round, when the gentlemen indulged in a grossness and profanity in conversation which are happily unknown at the present day.

CHAPTER 14

LIFE AT PITTSTON

In May, 1804 [before my marriage], I returned from the South to renew my labours in this place. Most of the spring and summer was occupied in completing the arrangements with the settlers, which were necessarily suspended by the cold weather in the early part of the preceding winter. An important duty also occupied much of my thoughts, the measures that were best adapted for the development of the natural advantages of the place. Unfortunately I had no experience on the subject, and those who from local knowledge were most capable of giving advice, were interested to induce me to make large expenditures. One of the pressing wants seemed to be a public house for the reception of travellers coming here on business. This I at once supplied by repairing and fitting up a large building erected by my grandfather before the American Revolution. It was the exact counterpart of the old court house built about the same time and still standing on the bank of the river in Dresden. Tho' originally well and substantially built, it was in a dilapidated state, the boards and clapboards of the lower story having been torn off by the occupants of the upper rooms for kindling wood. This I fitted up into a respectable country tavern. It stood on the same spot where is now the Gardiner Hotel.

The same season I built a fulling mill, which paid a fair rent for many years and brought business to the place.

I also commenced the great wharf, which cost $6000, and was an injudicious expenditure. It had a very large surface designed for piling lumber, but anyone acquainted with the river could have told me that there were freshets at almost all seasons of the year, which made it unsafe to allow lumber to remain on the wharves for any length of time. The wharf was also so situated as to be swept by the current in freshets, which carried off the gravel, depositing it in the docks below. The store houses, erected upon it were repeatedly carried away by the ice, tho' after each disaster I was at additional expense to make them more secure.

The expense of keeping the wharf and docks in good order has far exceeded all the income that has been derived from it. A small wharf costing only $500 or $600 might have been made advantageous.

About this time my father, having become somewhat embarrassed in his circumstances, partly from the failure of Mr. Charles Vaughan and partly from his family expenses exceeding his income, was induced by Mr. Charles Vaughan to sell his very extensive and valuable real estate in Boston to some speculators who built Broad Street and Central Wharf. The plans of the estate were burnt up in my office. There must have been several hundred feet on Battery March Street, extending to the water, and the garden and pasture round the house must have contained 3 or 4 acres. $40,000 were paid for the shipyard etc., and $20,000 for the house, garden, and pasture.

The sale of the house and garden was not necessary to the relief of my father, nor to the plan for the new street and wharves. If it had been retained, its real value would have been very greatly enhanced by the new street, and would at this time have been worth an immense sum. The speculators made no improvement on this part of the estate. The mansion house still stands as it was, and the garden has been sold in house lots. The arrangements were made while I was absent to the south, tho' not completed till my return.

Upon arriving at Kennebec with your mother [in 1805], I at once took possession of the house which my father had built in Pittston on the Worromontogus tract bequeathed to my mother, immediately in front of the Gardiner ferry. The house was small and only a story and a half high, and was planned by Charles Vaughan as a summer residence for my father and without conveniences for a family. It is still standing, and is now in the occupation of the widow of Caleb Stevens*. My father usually came down about the

*Removed to Oaklands in 1927 and now called the Hallowell Cottage.

HALLOWELL COTTAGE

Built by Robert Hallowell 1796

Removed to Oaklands 1927

middle of June and remained three or four months, and we went up to him for a longer or shorter time as my business permitted. Your grandmother had brought up her children in great seclusion. They had been instructed by masters at home, never having been at any school, and their visiting was extremely limited. But the seclusion of a town residence was very different from our solitariness in Pittston. The river cut us off from all neighbors, the crossing of which, under the most favorable circumstances, was unpleasant, for it was very difficult to keep the log canoe in which we crossed dry and clean. We kept up a weekly dinner intercourse with the Vaughans at Hallowell, meeting alternately at Hallowell and Pittston as the tide suited, for we were obliged to go by water in a sailboat. It rarely happened when they were to come to us, that they did not delay setting off beyond the time I had given them, and that I was obliged to send men to meet them and assist them against the tide. As the roads improved, wheels were substituted for the boat, but then we had to cross in a gondola, and once, as we started from the shore, my horse became restive and was backing the chaise upon your mother, when she jumped into the river. Fortunately we were only a few feet from the shore, where the water was quite shallow, but of course our visit was interrupted.

Occasionally we had a visitor from Boston. My business occupied much of my time and thoughts. I had no clerk and kept my own books, and I could not always get through what was to be done before dinner, and more than once forgot to send over the provisions necessary for that repast. Your mother therefore had many lonely hours, particularly in the spring and autumn months when the old Squire was engaged in his surveys and I was obliged to devote my evenings to plotting down the work he had accomplished the preceding day.

The autumn of 1805 had faded away into stern winter before I was able to take your mother to make our visit to my father in Boston, and her expected confinement prevented her returning with me when my business required my presence here in the spring. I made my visit as short as possible, and then returned to Boston to await the expected joyous event. I became a parent. What emotions does the first realization of the relation excite? The affection of a father for his child is very different from that of a husband for his wife, but who shall say which is strongest? The deep affection for my first born was fully reciprocated, and the response to my enquiry of her feelings on the morning when she exchanged the abode of her earthly parent for that of the Heavenly Father, accompanied by the sweetest smile, can never be effaced from my memory. 'I am better, dear father.' With these words her consciousness departed, and she went to her rest without a groan.

Emma, from her earliest childhood, ever was the most truthful and conscientious child I ever knew, and though her whole life was spent in doing her Master's will, she considered social intercourse as consistent with her duty to God, and made herself very agreeable in society. Anne was born in the same house in Elliott Place on the 10th December of the following year. Your sister Emma was born in Boston, May 29th, 1806, a short time before the memorable total eclipse of June in that year. It was a sad disappointment that your mother was not able to leave her chamber to see it. If I had been previously aware of the very striking appearance of the phenomenon, which would not be seen here again for a period of eighty years, I should have endeavoured to have had some kind of litter made for her to be taken where it was visible. The time of peculiar interest was when the sun became wholly hidden from sight. The light of day was instantly succeeded by the darkness of night. There was not a cloud in the heavens, and the stars everywhere appeared. The morning had been warm, but a damp chill immediately pervaded the atmosphere. The fowls went to roost, the cocks began to crow. The streets were full of people watching the progress of the eclipse, but when the last ray of the sun disappeared and the darkness succeeded instantaneously to the light of day, everyone seemed struck with awe. Men and animals stood motionless. There was not the slightest movement of any kind. It was as if some great magician with supernatural powers had, by the waving of his wand, suspended all the operations of nature. Astonishment and awe seemed depicted in every countenance. Soon the moon passed from before the sun, and restored to us his glorious light. His first ray gave cheerfulness to everyone, and by an involuntary impulse without premeditation, every hat was taken off from the immense crowds, and the air everywhere resounded with the most hearty cheers, and all returned to their accustomed occupations. It was a scene I should never forget should I live a hundred years. I have since seen an annular eclipse, which, though very interesting, did not approach in sublimity to that which I have just described.

In the spring of 1806, two Scottish Highlanders came here to seek a place of settlement for a body of their countrymen who had been driven from their homes. They had embarked for N. Carolina, where many of the Scotch were settled, but their vessel was driven by stress of weather into Boston. They were told that Maine was as advantageous a place of settlement for emigrants as North Carolina, that the climate more nearly resembled the one to which they had been accustomed, and that by coming here they would save much delay and expense. The two that came here were intelligent men and had the entire control and direction of the party. They alone spoke English. The others knew no tongue but their native Gaelic. We are all familiar with the beautiful descriptions in Scott's novels of the intercourse between the Highland chief and his clan, who were united by closer ties than have been known to exist in any other state of society, and while the ties continued, it would have been impossible by any inducements for the chief to sever those ties and to drive to foreign lands those who, for so many generations, had been closely united to him and his fathers. But the Scottish chief had been converted into the English gentleman. Educated at English schools and English universities, and residing most of the year in the southern kingdom, he had lost almost all interest in his ancestral domain, which he visited only for a short time in the sporting season. The faithful clansmen had become peasants, and, while accepting the high rents offered for their lands by English farmers, he thought their welfare would be really promoted by seeking a home in America. The acquisition of such a body of settlers seemed to me desirable, and as I had several small houses on the river bank in front of Oaklands, vacated by the squatters whose possession I had purchased, I offered to provide one-half of them with homes, and Mr. Vaughan, having several small houses built by his brother Charles for workmen, consented to provide accommodation for the other half. They were to pay no rent for the first year, till they could become acquainted with the country and provide for themselves. They were quite orderly people, members of the Scottish Kirk, and their leaders kept them strictly attentive to their religious duties. Never accustomed at home to do more than provide for their own scanty subsistence, they were very awkward and slow in learning our work, but business was then in its palmiest state, and inferior as was their labour, they found full employment, and every man received at night a silver dollar for his day's work. The women also found employment in washing, their mode of performing which was peculiar, and excited much amusement among our people. The operation was performed by the feet. The women, tucking their petticoats up to their knees, jumped into the tubs, which were placed in the road in front of their cottages, and kept the clothes in constant motion till they supposed the dirt was sufficiently squeezed out. The adage that cleanliness and good morals are closely associated did not apply in their case, for they were the filthiest people I ever met with. They were here spoiled by prosperity. In their own country they had been contented with earning four pence a day, living upon oaten cakes, and never seeing meat from year's end to year's end. Here they became dissatisfied with high wages and good living, because our people, performing more and better work, received higher wages than themselves. Towards the end of the following year they became so discontented that they said they must go down to King George's land. Their leaders went down to Nova Scotia and selected a location for them, and took them all down the next spring. The following season I received a letter from one of the leaders expressing great disappointment at their situation, and regretting exceedingly that they had gone away, and begging to be allowed to come back and be reinstated in the houses they had left. I replied that the buildings they had occupied had been either taken down or applied to other uses and could not be again offered to them, that they had remained here long enough to know the comparative advantages of Maine and Nova Scotia for emigrants, and, if they returned, it must be on their own responsibility. I never received any reply to this letter.

The winter of 1806-7 was well advanced before my business would allow me to leave and make our promised visit to my father. Before leaving I took your mother one calm afternoon to visit the Dumaresqs at Swan Island, ten miles below. The ice was smooth and we went with great rapidity, and enjoyed our visit, but were surprised to find on our return the thermometer at 30° below zero. Buffalo robes were then unknown. Your mother had a cloak wrapped round herself and Emma (then an infant between seven and eight months old), and a horse rug was the only protection for our feet, but we did not suffer from the cold. I only found some inconvenience from my eyelashes freezing together. This is another proof of the well-known fact that the human constitution will conform itself to the circumstances in which it is placed. People here fifty years ago did not suffer more in their thin clothes and open houses than they do now in houses heated with furnaces, and wrapped in furs when they ride out. The only place of public worship that was warmed in winter in those days in this country, and probably in the whole state, was our little church, and it was sneeringly said that the Episcopalians were obliged to have a stove in church, as they had not faith enough to keep themselves warm without. It is a consoling thought that the poor, unable to protect themselves from the rigours of the climate, become hardened to them and do not suffer from them, as we with our habits are sometimes disposed to believe they do.

It was about 1808 that a mail stage was established to run three times a week from Portland to Augusta through

Litchfield and West Gardiner. Our roads then did not permit its coming through the village, and we obtained our mail from the post office at Hallowell. At first it was brought in his pocket by any of our citizens who chanced to be coming from there, and afterwards we employed a boy to go for it regularly. A mail is of so much importance to the character as well as to the business of the place, that I set myself earnestly at work to have it pass through here directly. I had the route carefully surveyed, and then established by the court, and made a post route by Act of Congress. Only that portion of it in this town was made, but beyond, it passed for 3½ miles through a narrow strip in Litchfield, separated from the rest of the town by Pleasant Pond. Litchfield resisted making that part of the road, as they knew the strip would be set off to the adjoining town of Bowdoinham (now Richmond) as soon as the road should be constructed, and till then they would not allow the annexation. I was therefore obliged to attend from court to court, and make such representations as would induce the court to impose fines upon the town. These were laid out in making the road by persons appointed on my recommendation. I did not relax my efforts until the road was completed, at the end of about four years. Then Paine, the great mail contractor, was made to believe that the stage could not run upon it. I told him otherwise and asked him to examine for himself. Soon after he drove to my house early one morning and said to me in his rapid manner, 'I have examined your road—like it—you shall have the mail tomorrow—good morning.' We had it, and have ever since retained it, though an effort was made to have it restored to the old road. Baker, who kept a respectable public house on that road, about half way between Brunswick and Hallowell, had just built a new large public house for the accommodation of travellers, and found that his custom was taken away by the establishment of the new post road. He got up a petition for its restoration which was very numerously signed at Hallowell, professedly to save a worthy man from great loss, though I do not think there is any uncharitableness in supposing that jealousy of a rising rival village stimulated their sympathy for the worthy man. I was surprised to find on the petition the names of all my Hallowell friends, who must have known the importance of the mail route to this place, and to me personally.

I do not, however, forget the strong bias there always is upon people to act with the mass of the community among whom they are living, when the question of issue is supposed to involve the interest of that community.

In the spring of 1809 Solicitor Davis, when attending the Supreme Court in their circuit in Maine, brought with him his daughter Louisa, a pleasing young girl just entering upon life, with an unformed character. She accepted your mother's invitation to spend the summer with us, and she always remembered and gratefully acknowledged the benefit she had derived from your mother's friendly advice in the formation of her character. A friendship was formed between them during this visit which continued uninterrupted through life. She married William Minot, with whom I had been on intimate terms at school and at college. He was a man of the greatest uprightness in every relation of life, of warm feelings and cultivated taste, and our early friendship has become stronger as those who shared it with us in youth have been gradually removed, and we are nearly left alone. Their children were imbued with good principles, the sons holding highly respectable positions in society, the daughters unmarried, with feeble health, continuing in the paternal home, and all repaying to their surviving parent the attention bestowed upon them in early life, and making his declining years comfortable.

VAUGHAN

Parents	Children
SAMUEL VAUGHAN of London 1720-1802 m. Sarah Hallowell 1727-1809 daughter of Benjamin Hallowell of Boston	BENJAMIN VAUGHAN, M. D., M. P. 1751-1836 m. Sarah Manning of London 1753-1834 (Ancestors of the present Vaughans of Hallowell) WILLIAM VAUGHAN 1752-1850 JOHN VAUGHAN 1756-1842 ANN VAUGHAN 1757-1847 m. John Darby CHARLES VAUGHAN 1759-1839 m. Frances W. Apthorp SARAH VAUGHAN 1761-1818 unmarried SAMUEL VAUGHAN 1762-1802 REBECCA VAUGHAN 1766-1851 m. John Merrick 1766-1862 Also three children who died in infancy

CHAPTER 15

THE VAUGHAN FAMILY

The society of Hallowell was principally distinguished from the Vaughan connection. The two brothers Benjamin and Charles were sons and Mrs. Merrick a daughter of my father's oldest sister who married Mr. Samuel Vaughan, a London merchant owning a very valuable plantation in Jamaica where he resided with my aunt for several years after their marriage. My aunt was a lady of much dignity of character and the greatest kindness of disposition—which made her children and friends warmly attached to her—and of strong common sense. Mr. Vaughan was engaged in some commercial transactions with my grandfather which proved unfortunate. He was a strong Whig in politics and is noticed in Junius' letters. After his return to England he entered heartily into party strife and election contests which he found drew so heavily upon his purse that he had the prudence to withdraw from them before his fortune had suffered materially. He became intimately acquainted with Dr. Franklin and other leading characters of our Revolution and took very strong interest in the prosperity of our country which he believed would become great and prosperous, and inspired his children with a strong attachment to America. He brought all his family out to this country two years after the peace [of 1783].

John remained in Philadelphia where he carried to its full extent the family trait of public spirit and active benevolence. Never incumbering himself with a wife and family, he devoted himself wholly to the public, calling upon all strangers who came to the city, attending to their wants and introducing them to society and showing them everything worthy of observation. He, with two other merchants, established the Unitarian Society in that city, and for some years they conducted the service in rotation till it fell altogether upon Mr. Taylor. While Mr. Vaughan was conducting the service, Mr. Buckminster's sermons were published in Boston, and he had the sheets as printed sent to him by mail that he might read them to his congregation before they were known to the public. He lived to an advanced age and few persons had a larger circle of friends to mourn their departure.

Charles settled in Boston and married Miss Fanny Apthorp a lady of great beauty and uncommon sweetness of disposition. She and her sister were orphans, and had been educated in the greatest seclusion in the same city by doting grandparents. Their residence was in a house situated in a large garden surrounded by a high brick wall, the limits of which they rarely passed, and an English maid always attended them in their walks around the garden or while they were sitting pensively watching the growth of their flowers or listening to the singing of the birds. Their grandfather bequeathed to these ladies large fortunes which he endeavored to secure to them, but in both cases unsuccessfully. Mr. Vaughan commenced business in Boston at a time of its greatest prosperity and under peculiar advantages, his father affording him credit to a very large amount, and the trustees of his wife's property allowing him the use of it. He engaged very extensively in the China trade at a time when almost all concerned in it were making large fortunes. He engaged in land and building speculation in Boston and besides his large expenditures and schemes at Hallowell he attempted to make a town at Jones' Eddy, seven miles below Bath, and speculated very extensively in wild lands and failed with a very large indebtedness. My father was on his paper to a much larger amount than the whole of his property. Mr. Vaughan assigned to him and his wife's brother Apthorp, also his endorser, a ship called the Frances and Mary (names of his wife and her sister) and her cargo coming from China. It was then thought that a simple bill of sale without actual delivery was not sufficient to transfer the title to a ship, but a handsome fee to the pilot kept the ship below till she could be formally transferred. After his failure Mr. C. Vaughan retired to a farm in Hallowell, for whose prosperity he had formerly done so much, where he built a neat cottage. It was unfortunately situated in a low damp meadow, the miasma from which produced much ill health in his family. Mrs. Vaughan, retiring from a life of luxury and great indulgence, submitted with cheerful resignation to the privation and inconveniences of her new situation where good domestics were not to be obtained and sometimes none of any kind. Strong domestic affections were cultivated in the children with firm principles, forming them for useful citizens and making a happy home. Mr. Vaughan acted for some years as an agent for several landed proprietors, for my grandfather Hallowell's estate and for the Plymouth Co., an office at that time, when the squatters were at war with the proprietors, of much labour and expense. He subsequently engaged in manufacturing in a small way and again failed. He wanted the exactness and method which are essential to success in business. This want of success prevented a due appreciation in Hallowell of what he had done for the town, notwithstanding which he continued ever ready to engage in whatever would promote the prosperity of the place. His figure was well proportioned and his features regular, and the kindliness of his disposition, expressed so forcibly in his countenance, joined with his urbanity and gracefulness of manners made him many strong friends. After his wife's death his youngest son and family came to reside with him and he died in a good old age with affectionate sons to close his eyes.*

Samuel, the youngest son, subsequently went to Jamaica as agent of the family estates.

Benjamin was the oldest of the family. He was educated at Cambridge University in England, enjoying all its advantages except that being a Unitarian he could not subscribe to the 39 Articles which at that time was necessary

*Note of R. H. G. 2nd.

But a very few years before his death, Mr. Vaughan engaged in a speculation for forming a water power and building mills at the mouth of the St. John near the City of St. John. John Otis, who was also interested, went down to look after the concern having full power of attorney from Mr. V. Otis, believing the bubble would soon burst, as it did, sold out the whole property at a small profit. At this Mr. Vaughan was much annoyed and lamented the sale.

to matriculation and to obtaining of a degree. Mr. Vaughan engaged the affections of Miss Manning, the daughter of a rich London merchant, but her father would not consent to the marriage until he had means of his own for the support of a family. To gain his wife, Mr. Vaughan went to Edinburgh to study medicine, where he remained two years, and after receiving his degree of doctor of medicine, obtained the object of his affections. Mr. Vaughan was a man of very great learning, and there were few subjects with which he was not well acquainted. He had no originality of thought but possessed a very retentive memory, but he cramped the power of his own mind by dwelling too much upon the thoughts of others. He had an extensive library, and his books were marked in about every page so that he could refer at once to the authorities he wanted, and in conversation, of which he was very fond, taking the largest share to himself, he generally gave the opinion of others on the topics discussed rather than what he thought himself.

After his marriage, Mr. Manning took him as partner into his house, doing a large and lucrative business with the West Indies, and Mr. Vaughan's duty was to conduct the correspondence which was extensive, and the heads of which were furnished to him by the senior partner. He had formerly been private secretary to Lord Shelburne, and through his interest obtained a seat in Parliament and became intimately associated with the leading Whigs. After the surrender of Lord Cornwallis at Yorktown, the British Government abandoned all hope of reducing the rebellious colonies to obedience and the people became clamorous for peace. A negotiation between revolted colonies and the mother country was one of a peculiar and delicate nature and Lord Shelburne, then Prime Minister, knowing that Mr. Vaughan, his former secretary, was deeply interested in the American cause and was on intimate and confidential terms with all the distinguished Americans who had been in England, and particularly with Dr. Franklin, one of the negotiators, consulted him as to the proper person to be appointed by the British government to meet the American commissioners. Upon his recommendation, Richard Oswold, a London merchant engaged in trade with America, was appointed, but in the accounts of the negotiations which Oswold afterward published, he showed himself very inferior in talent to either of the three Americans, Franklin, Adams or Jay. Lord Shelburne also engaged Mr. Vaughan to act as a confidential messenger during the whole negotiation and to continually pass between Paris and London; personally explaining what it was not thought proper to commit to writing. One of the greatest difficulties in commencing the negotiations was a matter of form and pride. The English government were willing in the treaty to acknowledge the independence of the revolted colonies, but the Americans would not consent to treat but as the ambassadors of a free and sovereign state. It was long before the British would consent to yield this point which, however, they at length did. Mr. Manning was a high Tory and for the part that Mr. Vaughan, his son in law, took in this business, he cut him off from the profits of the house for a year. With Dr. Priestly and most of the English Unitarians, Benjamin Vaughan had adopted republican opinion and hailed with delight the first dawning of the French Revolution, being fascinated with the ideal notions of the French philosophers of the purity and simplicity of man in his unsophisticated state. Mr. Vaughan was invited with Mrs. Vaughan and other English of the same opinions, to be present at the opening of the first French national convention, which was to inaugurate a new era in the history of hitherto benighted man, which invitation they accepted. Many of these enthusiasts, believing that a democracy was the most perfect form of government and that it was calculated to promote the happiness of every people where it was introduced, were desirous that England should be revolutionized and converted into a democratic republic, which they thought might be easily effected with the assistance of a small body of troops from France, and for this purpose entered into correspondence with some of the leaders of the French Revolution. Several of these persons were arrested, tried and transported. Upon one of them named Stone, a letter was found from Mr. Vaughan dissuading from the attempt to introduce French troops. As soon as Mr. Vaughan heard that a letter of his had been found upon Stone, he instantly fled to France and took refuge with Mr. Skipworth, the American consul at Paris. Mr. Skipworth gave him the use of his country house, where Mr. Vaughan considered himself in concealment, although he was freely visited by many of the leading politicians and savants residing in Paris. Mr. Vaughan's brother-in-law Manning was a member of Parliament and a supporter of government. He applied to Mr. Pitt to know in what light Mr. Vaughan's conduct was viewed by Government, and whether he might safely return to England. Mr. Pitt replied that the government perfectly understood Mr. Vaughan's character, that they considered him as an enthusiast but in no respect a dangerous person, and that he would assure him that Mr. Vaughan might return to England with perfect security without having the slightest apprehension that the government would take any notice of what had occurred. Mr. Vaughan, believing himself of great political importance, placed no confidence in these assurances, thinking that Mr. Pitt was only laying a trap to get him into his power. He, therefore, determined to expatriate himself and come to the United States. As the war between France and England prevented direct intercourse between the two countries, Mr. Vaughan directed his family to leave England for America under the care of Mr. Merrick, a tutor in his family. They came to Boston and took a house in what is now Brighton. In about a year Mr. Vaughan, without ever again visiting England, followed them to this country and settled at Hallowell on the family lands.

This family added very much to the society of the place. Mr. Vaughan interested himself very much in the prosperity of the country, but particularly of Hallowell. He was at great expense in importing improved breeds of animals and new fruits, and spared no expense on his farm and orchard which, unfortunately, were not on a good soil. He also made use of his medical education in the cause of benevolence, and practised very extensively as a consulting physician, but as his advice was gratuitous and he did not wish to be overburdened with practice nor to interfere with the emoluments of the regular physicians of the place, he would not visit but in company with one of them. He had an extensive medical library, to which were added the most valuable and recent medical works immediately after they were published in England, which he regularly imported and the use of which was freely permitted to the physicians of the place. As a consulting physician his advice was frequently very valuable.

Mrs. Vaughan was never reconciled to her expatriation. From the miniatures of her she must have been very handsome in her youth. She possessed a lively wit, had read a great deal and had very agreeable powers of conversation and great kindness of disposition, being constantly engaged in kind actions to her neighbors. Though she had imbibed some of the visionary notions of her husband, they were restrained in her by practical good sense. When they were emigrating to America, Mr. Vaughan, wishing to conform to what he supposed to be the simple habits of the country, was desirous of selling all their plate, but Mrs. Vaughan's good sense enabled them to retain what was found in every family in the country, their silver spoons and their candlesticks.

Mr. and Mrs. Vaughan had both speculative notions of education derived from Rousseau and other French writers of that period, but they were not based on principles tested by experience. Their children were never allowed to go to school, but were instructed by private tutors residing in the family, and with the exception of Mr. Merrick who left the family when the children were young, the other tutors were strange beings selected for some particular acquisition or talent without the manners of gentlemen, with little common sense and no power of commanding the attention or respect of their pupils. The girls acquired some education from their mother, the boys some from the society that frequented their father's house, but they had less drilling and less power of study than many of the boys in the street.

After the residence of a few years in this country and witnessing the practical working of our democratic institutions, Mr. Vaughan became gradually weaned from the visionary theories he had so warmly embraced in Europe. He became a warm Federalist and zealous conservative.

Feeling that his banishment arose from an imprudent expression of his political feelings, he professed to live here as a philosopher, undisturbed by the party strife which raged around and tho' he had become a naturalized citizen, he could never be induced to appear at the polls on election days. He had, however, so long been accustomed to the excitement of political life he could not abstain from it here, and he wrote for the Boston newspapers and also some pamphlets upon the absorbing topics, taking great pains that the author should not be known. They were copied by persons whose writing should not be known and then passed circuitously to the printer. He allowed his boys to clear up and make a farm on the family property, two miles from the river, without any restraint as to the plans or expense, and they told me themselves that they had expended upon it, in the course of a few years, $70,000. Unfortunately the soil was very shoal upon a ledge of rock, and withal very stony, and could not, therefore, be made productive. This expenditure was an encroachment on the family property.*

Mrs. Vaughan had brought her husband a large fortune which was placed in her brother's hands as trustee, who, at the joint request of Mrs. Vaughan and her children, advanced Mr. Vaughan, at various times, large sums of the trust property. The misfortunes of the West India planters caused the failure of Mr. Manning, by which a large portion of Mrs. Vaughan's fortune was lost.

We were on intimate terms with the family and exchanged visits once or twice a week.* With all Mr. Vaughan's public

*Notes of R. H. G. 2nd.

Upon this farm there was an extensive orchard, the trees of which were all imported from England. It was supposed till then that the climate of Maine was too cold for apples. The soil of this orchard was very thin, lying on the top of a ledge, and it was necessary in summer to water many of the trees to keep them alive. Cider was made on an extensive scale, and this required expensive buildings, with constant fires in winter to keep the apples and cider from freezing. Large sums also were expended in importing stock.

*All the fortune of Mrs. Vaughan remaining at her death was 1000 shares of U. S. Bank valued at $120,000. This by will dictated by Mr. Vaughan was divided equally between Sally, Petty, Mrs. Emmons and Mrs. Grant. Not long after the famous contest between General Jackson and the bank began, which resulted finally in the annihilation of the bank. Such was the infatuation of the owners of the stock that a large portion of them made a total loss, not realizing that what

spirit and benevolence, vanity marred the beauty of his character. William was his favorite child. He thought so highly of his ability that he was in the habit of quoting as authority his opinions upon affairs of business whether public or private, but when William failed, Mr. Vaughan was mortified that he had been mistaken in his son's talents. His love was at once changed into hate, and he make his wife on her death bed, when her consciousness was nearly gone, execute a will by which William's children were disinherited.

Mr. Vaughan's manners were courteous, but there was a deference in them which resulted from his intercourse in the early period of his life in England with persons of a higher rank in society than himself, and which contrasted strongly with the independence of our American habits. Mr. Vaughan lived to an advanced age and was buried in the family burial ground in front of his mansion.

I necessarily was on intimate terms with Mr. Vaughan's children. The oldest son, William, was a year younger than myself, and we were thrown much together, tho' our views of life differed materially. He had natural abilities rather above the average, and a most determined will, with great daring and undaunted courage and strong taste for military life. If he had been indulged in entering the British army, where his taste led him, he would have made a very distinguished officer, but the finest points of his character had no scope for development in Hallowell, where the thoughts and feelings of the people ran in a totally different channel from his own.

The second son, Henry, gave promise of becoming a fine man, but he was lost overboard in early manhood.

Petty, the youngest, lived in Hallowell till towards the

was formerly a Bank of the United States had upon the expiration of its charter become a state bank. Father induced Mrs. Emmons to make him a loan of her shares, she however insisting upon the condition of his returning the stock if desired, and she thus saved $16,000. Mr. Grant sold out his wife's share in time to realize about the same amount, but Mr. Petty Vaughan, with the infatuation of other Englishmen, held onto his own and Sally's, till in answer to his nephew's repeated remonstrance he guaranteed that the stock should not fall below its then value, and the result was that both portions united produced for Sally about $8,000.

age of 40, when he went to London and engaged in business with his uncle and became involved in his uncle's failure. With less capacity than either of his brothers, he had a very uncommon kindliness of disposition, and very few Americans visited London during his residence there that did not experience the benefit of his attention. He died a bachelor in poverty.

An English gentleman by the name of Shepperd was sent out to Mr. John Vaughan of Philadelphia with a request that he would find some employment for him. John sent him to his brother Charles, who, not knowing how otherwise to employ him, sent him to Hallowell to establish a brewery. Shepperd was supposed to have connexions in high life in England, and his notions were all upon a grand scale, and in all his employments he deemed large expenditures necessary for the honour of his employer. He laid out his plans upon the scale of a London brewery. The cellar extended several hundred feet across the whole width of Bombahook Point. It never occurred either to Shepperd or Mr. Vaughan that there was but little barley raised in this country and that malt liquors were then but little used in New England. The digging of the cellars was commenced late in the autumn, and, to keep the ground from freezing, fires were kept up night and day. It is not necessary to say how such a concern must terminate. Shepperd had largely exceeded his allowance and was in debt to Mr. Vaughan. In the final settlement of their accounts, when Mr. Vaughan disputed some of the items and charges, Shepperd replied with perfect nonchalance, "Mr. Vaughan, we are both bankrupts, but if it gives you any satisfaction, as it will make no difference to either of us, I am perfectly willing that you should add a cipher to the debit side of my account."

*Note of R. H. G. 2nd.

When Petty went to England he was invited to make a visit to the old friends of his father, the Marquis and Marchioness of Landsdowne. Up to that period he had never been accustomed to walking. In going from his father's to the post office, ¼ of a mile, he never walked. The day after his arrival, the Marchioness proposed to him to take a little walk with her, and she walked 12 miles. Poor Petty thought it would kill him, but felt obliged to keep up with a lady.

His wife was an amiable, accomplished, and agreeable woman and sang very sweetly. They lived in a long low house on the bank of the river near the brewery. My sister was fond of her, and during the last summer vacation that I spent with her in Pittston, I used to paddle her up in my canoe to pass an afternoon there.

Mr. Merrick, another of the Vaughan connection, was educated under the celebrated Dr. Belsham for the Unitarian ministry. He came out to this country with Mrs. Vaughan as a tutor to their children. While they resided at Brighton he preached a few times at the stone chapel in Boston, but tho' a fine writer and able to express his thoughts with great force, and an uncommonly good reader, his pulpit performances were not popular, and he relinquished the design of becoming a clergyman. Soon after the family removed to Hallowell, he went to England to be married to the youngest sister of Mr. Vaughan, and making but a short stay there, he returned with his wife to Hallowell where he established himself on a farm on the family property. Mrs. Merrick made a most excellent wife and mother and the children all became estimable characters. Mr. Merrick was a man of highly honorable character, of fine mind and refined taste, particularly in music of which he was passionately fond. He had an exquisite sense of the ridiculous which he could not always restrain, even where it was inappropriate, but tho' he indulged it in early life, his natural kindness of disposition taught him subsequently not to display it to the annoyance of others. His knowledge, tho' not profound, embraced most subjects, particularly natural science, and he had acquired sufficient acquaintance with anatomy to perform simple surgical operations when a regular practitioner could not be procured. Not having any regular business, he was ever ready to assist his friends in anything useful or agreeable. I was desirous of obtaining a true meridian line by the north star for the purpose of setting a dial, and he proffered his assistance, and as our operations were repeatedly interrupted by a gust of wind, he repeated his visits, tho' after our social supper he had to cross the river in a boat and ride more than four miles to his own home. With his love of music he had acquired a great skill in chanting before leaving England, which was then but little practiced here, and he came for several seasons twice a week for some time before Christmas to drill our choir, and as there were several fine voices among them, we had, under his tuition, better chanting than was found in many city churches. Ostenelli and other distinguished musicians were attracted by him to spend their summer vacations partly or wholly in Hallowell, and he always brought them down to our house for your mother's gratification.

He was fond of listening to Ostenelli while accompanying with the violin your mother on the piano. He preferred your mother's performance, where he said she put her soul into the music, to the more artistic music of your Aunt Delia. He gave several of my children lessons in elocution, which had been one of his favorite studies, and under his instruction their reading was greatly improved. Their daughter Harriet was a great deal at our house, particularly at the time when Mr. Olney was with us. She then embraced those deep views of religion which her father did not receive till late in life, and which have enabled her to support, with perfect cheerfulness and resignation, intense bodily sufferings and helplessness, which have continued almost without intermission for a very long period. She had great sweetness of disposition and perfect unselfishness, so that we became much attached to her and felt to her as a daughter.

Your sister Delia spent one winter in their family while we were in Boston. They became very fond of her, and she reciprocated their regard.

Mrs. Merrick had not many personal attractions, but to great kindliness of disposition she added good principles and excellent common sense, which, if they did not make her brilliant, enabled her to become an excellent wife and mother. Their niece, Mary R. Merrick, whom they had adopted, was also a great deal in our family and made herself very agreeable.

CHAPTER 16

THE DUMARESQ FAMILY

My cousin, James Dumaresq, quite an original character, lived at Swan Island, within visiting distance. My aunt left three sons and two daughters. The two oldest sons entered the British navy. The daughters both married Scotch gentlemen, and I shall have occasion to speak hereafter of their children. James always boasted of being fellow midshipman on board the same ship with the 3rd son of George 3rd, afterwards King William 4th. While the ship was lying at Bermuda, he obtained a furlough to visit my uncle, John Gardiner of Pownalboro, but, overstaying his leave of absence, he lost his position in the navy. My uncle then put him into the store of Shepperd, the agent of C. Vaughan at Hallowell. As characteristic of him, it was said that he would regulate the price of the goods according to the pretty look of his female customers. When I asked if this was true, he would reply, 'O no. It would not be right to sell goods to the pretty girls below their value, but I did love to tuck it on to the ugly ones.'

As he had been more about the world than the young men of the place, he became a beau, and acquired the affections of a handsome daughter of Squire Farwell. My father thought that James wanted stability of character to make a good head of a family, and with his little property, without industrious habits, he would find it difficult to support a family. Other friends joined to discourage the match, but the young people were not disposed to listen to lessons of prudence. James exchanged some of the land bequeathed to him in Pittston for a farm that my grandfather had made on Swan Island, and which was included in his bequest to J. S. J. Gardiner, where he took his wife to a house built by my grandfather, and which is still standing, and depended upon his stalwart arm to provide from it a living for his family. The soil of his farm was fortunately very good, his wants were small, and there he lived contentedly. His spirits were exuberant, and, as he never thought of the morrow, he was never depressed.

He was a keen sportsman, and the passage of a flock of ducks would cause the oxen to be left in the furrow, and, when he saw a wild animal pass, he would in his eagerness thrust his gun thro' the window tho it might have to remain unmended for weeks.

We visited in the summer by water, and in the winter on the ice. When Emma was only 8 months old, I took your mother there in an open sleigh with only a rug to cover us, for furs had not then come into use, and when we got back we found the thermometer at 30 below zero, and yet neither your mother or the baby suffered from the cold. The only inconvenience that I felt was the difficulty of keeping my eyes open, from the freezing of the eyelashes. At this time scarcely more than half the clothing was worn that is now deemed necessary. The houses were very open, furnaces and double windows unknown, and yet people did not seem to suffer from the cold more than they do now.

When Dumaresq visited us, he always came for several days, and in the season always brought a fine bunch of wild fowl.

As my children became old enough, they welcomed his visits with great pleasure, and he kept them in a little back room perfectly delighted with the kites or toys he made, or stories he told, and no holiday was so agreeable to them as a few days at Swan Island. His large kitchen chimney was sufficiently capacious for square logs as seats beside the fire, on which Hallowell and his son Philip would sit in the cool evenings of autumn, listening eagerly to his stories of naval experience or sporting adventures, at times varied by his violin. There was something original in their life, from the master down to the cat and dog, who ate out of the same platter, each lifting up a paw to ward off encroachment, and the tame grey squirrels, who would spring from the shoulders of their friends on to the back of their supposed natural enemy, darting away when the intrusion would seem to be resented.

Without apprehension for the morrow, or regret for the

past, he was always cheerful, and, with unbounded generosity of feeling, he had a delicate sense of the honor of a gentleman. He always spent his Christmas with us, but never left home till the large Yule log had been put on the kitchen fire. It was selected in the summer from the finest white oak tree, irrespective of the price it would bring in the market for timber. One season late in the winter, he took his wife and children in a sleigh to her father's in Vassalboro, and, as he had no one to take care of his cattle during his absence, he turned them into the barn yard with as much hay as he thought they would want while he was gone, and with snow for their drink. A violent rain and thaw coming on detained him beyond the time fixed for his return, and, fearing for his cattle, he determined to return on skates, notwithstanding the urgent remonstrances of his friends, who told him that the ice had become wholly unsafe. Their remonstrances were of no avail, and he reached the island, tho' word was taken to his wife that he was lost, by persons who declared that they had seen him break thro' the ice and disappear. In the autumn of 1826 he had been spending some days with us, and the fourth day, after dinner, he said that he was going home. As it was blowing very heavily N. W. with squalls, I begged him to remain till the following day, but the more I urged him to stay, the more determined he seemed to go, and would answer my arguments by saying that a man that is born to be hung will never be drowned. I went with him to the landing to see him off. On account of the high wind he had put an extra quantity of ballast into his boat, and, as he left the shore, called out 'you will hear from me at Swan Island or at the bottom of the river.' Mrs. Tudor was sitting in the south chamber watching the boat. Her eyes were turned away for a minute, and when she looked out again, the boat was no longer visible. She supposed it had gone behind the point, but it was not long before some men came running to the house to say that he was drowned. A flaw had struck the boat, which immediately filled and sank. As Dumaresq was an excellent swimmer, notwithstanding his heavy clothing, he might possibly have reached the eastern shore, but he saw some men with a boat on the western and swam towards them, but the boat was aground, and before it could be launched, the short waves thrown into his face had stifled him and he sank.

I was going the next day to the General Convention of the church, for which my trunk was packed, but I staid to try and find his body, but we searched in vain, tho' we recovered the boat with the violin. His son Philip was then at sea and returned the following July, after seven years absence, and the same day his body floated ashore at Dresden, a remarkable coincidence, but readily accounted for. As long as the water remained cold the body was unchanged, but when the summer sun warmed it, the gases were developed and the body floated. I had it put in a coffin, the funeral service said over it, and placed in our tomb near the church, where it remained for several years.

It is remarkable how fatal the water has been to his family. His brother, just promoted to a captaincy in the British navy, was drowned coming ashore from his ship in Portsmouth harbour. His daughter-in-law and granddaughter were drowned in front of his house at Swan Island, and his son was drowned by falling from a steamer in Long Island Sound.

CHAPTER 17

SETTLING ESTATES

The heirs of my grandfather Hallowell were preparing at this time for a settlement of his estate. He had been dead more than 30 years, and no account had been exhibited at probate. The troubles of the Revolution, and the expatriation of both the executors, had prevented an early settlement. But when my uncle Benjamin, joint executor with my father, spent six months in the house with him in 1796-7, there was no reason why the settlement of the estate should not then have been closed, but the great aversion of both brothers to business. That aversion of my father had not been lessened in the succeeding ten years. During my grandfather's illness and after his decease, as my uncle was wholly absorbed in the political agitations of the day, the business of the estate devolved upon my father till both executors became absentees. My father kept no regular set of books, but the account to be prepared for probate had to be made out from memoranda in pocket books and loose receipts and papers, together with a mass of mixed papers, the greater part of no importance, and which filled two large chests. Mr. Charles Vaughan, one of the heirs, kindly agreed to assist me in the labours. We were several weeks engaged in it, and tho' the weather was cold, we needed no other fire but the useless papers that we burnt. The account as completed exhibited a large balance due to my father, and it was sent to the heirs in England for approval. They objected to the charge of interest for the long period since the debt had accrued, an objection not unreasonable considering the long delay in settling the estate. Mr. Charles Vaughan induced them to reconsider their proposal of discharging the balance in cash, and to insist that the payment should be made in land by an assignment of such portions of my grandfather's eastern lands as should be agreed upon. The account at probate was closed, and the amount due my father fixed, but owing to a very intricate deed of trust from Mr. Samuel Vaughan and my aunt for the benefit of their children, it was two or three years before the lands to be assigned could be agreed upon, and proper conveyances made. Family meetings were required, at which Mr. Benj. Vaughan attended as agent for my aunt Gould and Uncle Benjamin's heirs, and Mr. Charles Vaughan and Mr. Merrick for the Vaughan family. Mr. Wilde, as the counsel, always attended, and as there was always a dinner either at our house or Mr. Vaughan's, in which social intercourse occupied more time than business, they passed very pleasantly. I was urged very strongly by Mr. B. Vaughan to purchase my aunt Gould's and uncle Benjamin's shares of the eastern land, for which he was agent, which I finally consented to do, though it greatly added to my business.

About the same time a settlement was made at probate of my grandfather Gardiner's estate. Ten years previously Major Browne of the British Army and a son of my aunt had come out to this country to make inquiry into the state of his mother's interest in my grandfather Gardiner's property.

An account was then settled by the executors at probate and all the heirs, excepting those of my aunt Dumaresq, who were not in the country, without attending to the provisions of my grandfather's will in which he directed that his lands not specially devised should be sold by the executors and the proceeds equally distributed among his heirs, joined in a petition to the Supreme Court for a partition of those lands to be held in severalty. Commissioners were accordingly appointed who held respectable stations in the community, and doubtless meant to act impartially, but I doubt if so absurd a division was ever before made. They assigned to my sister and myself a strip of land in Hallowell 1¼ miles in length and four rods in width (the legal width of a public road), and to the heirs of my uncle John each a strip of land commencing in Fairfield and extending 15 miles from the river, and only 19 rods in width. In 1807 the illegality of this division, as directly at variance with the will, was discovered, and by legal advice, the executors conveyed to the several heirs the portions assigned to them by the commissioners, and as nothing was known about the heirs of Mrs. Dumaresq, the share that was left for her was conveyed to me in trust for their benefit.

Major Browne sold his mother's share to Messrs. Winthrop and returned to England. I immediately endeavoured to discover the heirs and devisees of my aunt Dumaresq. She had left two, both of whom had married Scotch gentlemen residing in the Bahamas, one of them, a Mr. Ferguson, a relative of the astronomer and nephew of Gillis, the historian of Greece, the other a Mr. Gow. Both daughters and their husbands had deceased. Mrs. Fergusom had left two daughters, one of them, Isabella, married to a Mr. Deane of Turks Island; the other single. In the course of a few months they received my letter informing them of the property I held in trust for their benefit, and Deane immediately came out with his wife and her sister. Their uncle, Francis Dumaresq, who had been guardian to his two nieces, took the opportunity of visiting his relations in this country, and came out with them. They arrived here in the spring of 1808, and, with the exception of a few weeks that Francis spent with his brother at Swan Island, and the rest of the family with Mrs. Powell in Boston, they were with us the whole summer.

I hardly know how we contrived to accommodate them all in our small cottage in Pittston, particularly as your uncle William [Tudor] was with us and my father came down at his usual time in July. He was always very good natured and obliging, and allowed two beds to be placed in his chamber, one of which was occupied by your uncle and the other by Francis Dumaresq, who shared his with James when he came up from the island. Francis was the exact counterpart of his brother James, the same thoughtlessness, the same good nature, the same restless activity, and the same exuberance of animal spirits. If Francis had ever possessed the same disinterestedness and the same kindliness, they had been deadened by the rude buffetings of a cold and selfish world. Your uncle could not avoid overhearing the conversation of the two brothers as they lay in bed before going to sleep, and he related to us one of their characteristic conversations.

They were talking very seriously about the nature of a future existence, of the reality of which they felt by no means certain. In the midst of it one of the brothers suddenly broke off the conversation by daring the other to try with him the next day to jump over a certain gate—so evanescent were their thoughts upon the most important subject. Isabella, the eldest of the sisters, was a gentle, pious, modest woman, very superior to her husband, who, though well meaning, was without education or intelligence. He had always resided at Turks Island, where the only occupation of the people is to make salt and catch turtle. He was so insensible to the beauties of nature, that when Mrs. Gardiner once pointed out to him some interesting scenery, he could only reply, 'I do not think they compare with the beauty of the glistening salt reflected on the white sand by the bright summer sun without a tree or shrub to intercept it.'

Both sisters were amiable. The younger, though unequal to her sister, resembled her in character. She was subsequently married to a Methodist clergyman, and settled in one of our south western states. During the summer I aided them in selling some of their lands in Hallowell, and as no other purchaser could be found for the remainder I bought them and in the autumn they returned to the Bahamas. While here they related their remarkable preservation from the effects of a very powerful hurricane which had occurred at Nassau when they were children. They were residing at the time of its occurrence with their uncle Ferguson on his plantation, in a substantial stone house. When the tempest threatened, the necessary precaution of shutting all the doors and windows to prevent its entrance had been neglected. An outside door facing the wind had been left open, and after the commencement of the storm no earthly power could close it. The compressed air soon tore the house to pieces and scattered a large portion of its fragments over the neighboring ocean. At the first threatening of danger some negro women servants in the house took the two little girls to the lee of a hillock, and lying with them flat on the ground, supported themselves by holding tight to some strong bushes while they held the children. They were thus saved from being blown away to inevitable destruction.

I learnt from them that their aunt and uncle Gow were both dead, leaving one son, heir to the other half of the Dumaresq property. They believed that he was residing in New Orleans. I entered into correspondence with him, and was eventually induced to purchase his interest in the lands I held in trust for $6000. When the last note for $2000 and interest became due, bills of exchange on New Orleans could not be obtained, and by Gow's order I enclosed the amount in bank notes in a letter and took evidence of its being duly deposited in the post office. A day or two afterwards the newspapers gave accounts of the mail having been stopped on two successive days in North Carolina and robbed of its contents, and though the money was at Gow's risk, I felt very anxious till I heard of its safe arrival. Some years afterwards Gow wrote to me that he had been unfortunate in business and had lost all his property, and asked me to find a situation for him here. Not knowing of his character or habits I could only reply that the openings for business were much better in Louisiana than in Maine, and that the prospect of obtaining business or employment must be better where he was known than here where he would be an entire stranger. I never heard from him again.

CHAPTER 18

OAKLANDS

As my family was increasing and my social relations enlarging, the cottage in Pittston in which I had resided four years was inadequate to our wants and to our comfort, and not appropriate to my position in society. I therefore determined to build a commodious house. My investment in improving the estate was large, but my extensive sales of land seemed to justify the expense of a comfortable residence. The land at Worromontogus, gradually sloping to the river with a fine view of the vessels sailing on it, made me think of building there, but the duty of being a citizen of the place where the bulk of my property was situated, and the convenience of being accessible to people wishing to see me on business, in addition to getting rid of constantly crossing an inconvenient ferry, determined me to build on this side the river. My friends at Hallowell were desirous that I should build north of the Cobbossee Contee, in order to be nearer to them, but I had sold several lots on the river front on which houses had been erected before I thought of building myself, so that I could no longer have had there the grounds that I wished around my house.

Forty acres of the land on which we now live I had sold to the Louds. Their object in making the purchase was to obtain the right of establishing a ferry on the west side of Kennebec River at the great thoroughfare between the country lying on the two sides of Kennebec River and known as Smith's Ferry. Failing in their object, and unable to meet the stipulated payments, they were very desirous that I should cancel the bargain and take back the land, of which I was equally desirous, as I had become satisfied that I could not find another place on the estate so well adapted to my residence, and the reconveyance was accordingly made. Much of the wood on the front had been cut off during my minority, and fires, kindled accidentally

FIRST HOUSE AT OAKLANDS

From a drawing by Emma Jane Gardiner

by sportsmen in the brushwood left on the ground, had injured the remaining trees. The Louds had done no work on the land but to cut down the bushes and a few of the injured trees. As soon as I had completed my repurchase of the Louds, in the autumn of 1808, I had the land from which they had cut the bushes ploughed, and engaged Elkanah McLellan to occupy one of the squatters' houses remaining on the place, till the farm house could be built, and carry on the place. McLellan was a man of intelligence and great energy. He managed the place very well, and executed various pieces of business off the place with which I entrusted him with fidelity and judgment.* Unfortunately he was not equally faithful in his domestic relations, and his sons turned out miserably. The next year the farm buildings were put up. In the spring of that year Mr. John Richards made us a visit on his way to Machias, and as he was a gentleman of taste, familiar with the country residences of English gentlemen, I asked his assistance in selecting the exact spot where the house should be placed, to which he readily assented, and spy glass in hand, we climbed tree after tree to find the best view, and I do not think the location fixed upon, and on which the house is erected, could have been changed for the better.

When the house was framed, according to the custom of the country, I invited the neighbours to the 'raising', and as it was too large to be finished in half a day, I gave them a handsome cold collation under the trees, with a plentiful supply of good liquor, which was then thought necessary to draw out genial influences. Temperance laws had not then been thought of, and would not have been congenial to the temper of the times. The house was not complete for our occupation until the following year.*

*Note of R. H. G. 2nd.

When father returned from Boston in the spring of 1809, he found McLellan had built a wharf in front of Oaklands for the purpose of shipping wood by the coasters. This was of course immediately stopped, but the foundations of the wharf he built remain to this day.

One of the undertakings carried out successfully by McLellan was the moving of the stable to the village. A passage was cut through the oak woods, and with 60 yoke of oxen the stable was drawn up to the Brunswick Road on the snow, and then down Col. Stone's hill (Brunswick St.) In going down the hill all control was lost, and it was supposed the destruction of the building and the oxen was inevit-

November 3d, 1809, Hallowell, our first son, was born in the cottage in Pittston, where we had no neighbours, and where a river, cold and dreary at that season, separated us from the assistance necessary on such occasions. A boy (for we kept no man servant) had to be sent in the night in a log canoe across the river, first for the doctor and then again for the nurse. Neither of them arrived till the little stranger had made his appearance. Fortunately nature had done her part so kindly that your mother needed no other assistance than what I was able to afford.

We now had three children under 3½ years of age.

This rapid child bearing, with nursing and family cares, affected your mother's health, and she became subject to neuralgic pain in the face and tic doloreux, which affected her spirits and interfered with her enjoyment of society during the winter we spent in Boston. She had also to endure in my father's family the jealousy of his housekeeper, a most faithful woman, who had lived with him for a long course of years, and after the death of my mother and sister had taken the entire charge and control of his domestic arrangements. It was natural that the thought of this authority which she had so long enjoyed being taken from her, and a young mistress placed over her, should excite her, and make her show unpleasant feelings, but your mother pursued such a judicious and conciliatory course of conduct, interfering as little as possible with family arrangements, that this jealousy was after a time entirely subdued, and Sally Dodge eventually acquired a respect and sincere regard for your mother.

When my father came to live with us, as he was feeble and required much care, she devoted herself to his comfort to the close of his life. She had laid by a couple of thousand dollars while in my father's service, the interest of which, with an allowance of a dollar a week that I gave her, enabled her to live comfortably among her connections at

able, but McLellan by his great coolness in the midst of the panic put obstructions in front and saved the catastrophe. The building was placed on what is now Rogers corner, and was fitted up into two stores, one a bookstore occupied by Sheldon, and the other an apothecary occupied by Dr. Enoch Hale and his assistant James Bowman.

Ipswich, who treated her with respect from the expectation of inheriting her fortune.

In the autumn of 1810 the house at Oaklands was completed, and your mother and I went to Boston to purchase our furniture, and early in November we removed to Oaklands and greatly enjoyed our large premises, which not only afforded us accommodation for our rapidly increasing family, but rooms for the many guests who came to visit us.

We endeavoured to leave our visitors at liberty as much as possible, without forcing them to see sights in which they took no interest, and we had reason to believe that we made their sojourn agreeable. Many gentlemen now tell me of their visits to us which had entirely faded from my recollection. All the clergy visiting Gardiner invariably staid with us, so that one of our chambers acquired the name of the 'Minister's room'. If, however, they were engaged by the parish to preach for more than a Sunday or two, they left our house and took lodgings in the village.

Many of our guests were men of distinction, though not politicians. Those who made the deepest impression upon me, perhaps from seeing more of them alone, were Bishop Alonzo Potter and Chancellor Kent. Bishop Potter was then much engaged in the subject of education, and particularly upon the question of making it selfsupporting by uniting with it manual labour. I drove him in a chaise to the Methodist establishment at Kent's Hill, Readfield, where they made an exhibit by which it would appear that the articles made by the students sold for more above the cost of materials than was sufficient to pay their expenses. But upon close inquiry we found that the things made by the scholars were sold to friends of the institution, who, for its encouragement, were willing to pay higher than the market price for articles not so well made. I afterwards tried the experiment, fitting up a shop with water power, and charging no rent to the person who had charge of the lads, but it did not succeed. The truth is that young men who are striving for an education feel no interest in a mechanical employment which is to be of no use to them in after life, and the mechanic who takes apprentices whose desire it must be to learn the business upon which their future support is to depend, considers that for the first two years they scarcely earn their expenses. The labour of lads in a garden, directed by a master, and when no rent has to be paid, may yield a profit. I have rarely enjoyed so pleasant and profitable a day as this day's ride with Bishop Potter.

Chancellor Kent, with his exuberant flow of thought and language, was a great contrast to the slow and dignified manner of Bishop Potter. The chancellor had one of those inquiring minds which made him desirous of understanding everything and its cause, great or small, that came within his notice. His conversation was rich and full of thought, and flowing without an effort. He was very conservative and fully aware of the dangers arising from our democratic institutions. The convention for awarding the constitution of New York, of which he was a member, had just closed its sittings, and I asked him how it was that they should have continued that strange provision in their former constitution, that a judge should be superannuated at the age of 60. He replied, 'As I was just approaching that age, it would not have been proper for me to have opposed it. The other judges were mostly in the same situation. The members of the bar, who looked forward to taking our places, would not object to it, and the other members of the convention considered that if the judges and lawyers thought the provision proper it was not for them to object to it, and so it passed.' If Chancellor Kent had been continued on the bench, he would not have had time to write the able work on international law, which is as highly valued in England as in this country, and is made a text book in their colleges.*

*Note of R. H. G. 2nd.

In speaking of the various distinguished visitors beside those mentioned, Micheaux should not be forgotten. When engaged upon his beautiful work on American forest trees he spent some days at Oaklands. Not being able to draw or paint, he would secure the leaf of a tree to a sheet of paper, also the acorns or other seed vessels, and write a description, and with a dash of a brush give the colour of the leaf. Being desirous of adding some title to those he already possessed, Mr. Vaughan succeeded in reviving for the occasion a defunct agricultural society at Hallowell, and Micheaux was made a member and the society was again dissolved. On his return to Paris, Micheaux made a grand plantation of the seeds and trees he brought from America in which he took great pride. But one day Napoleon wanted the ground for parade, and all Micheaux's labours were swept away.

Among the agreeable visitors whom our large house enabled us to receive were the judges of the Supreme Court of Massachusetts, in its annual circuit in Maine. A week was appropriated for the law term in each county, which being more than sufficient for the law business in Kennebec County, there was always a day or two of leisure at the close of the week. The whole court dined with Mr. Vaughan on one Saturday and with us on the next. Judge Parker, being a relative of your mother's, always spent his spare time with us, as did one or two of the other judges. Lawyers by their profession have a close intercourse with a great variety of character, and acquire a greater insight into the motives which influence mankind than most other people. They are led into deep thinking, and necessarily acquire a fluency in expressing their thoughts, so that no class in the community form such pleasant members of society as those belonging to the bar. We always looked to the coming of the court as one of the most pleasing incidents of the year. This acquaintance with the judges of the Supreme Court led to my being generally invited to the meetings of the Law Club, when I spent my winters in Boston. The club consisted of the judges of the Supreme Court and some ten or twelve of the older and most distinguished members of the bar, and met every Monday evening. Law questions were seldom mooted, but the Club was not too large to admit of general conversation, which was always interesting, and the evening was closed with a supper. Among the members with whom I was more particularly acquainted were Judge Parker and Judge Jackson of the supreme bench, Judge Prescott, and Mr. John

Other visitors were Mr. Clark, afterwards Bishop of Rhode Island, Horatio Potter, Bishop of New York, Bishops Griswold, Chase of Ohio and Henshaw. Rev. James Richmond was a very frequent visitor. He was a graduate of Harvard of 1828, and a very remarkable man. He was a wonderful linguist; besides many other tongues he could converse fluently in Latin and modern Greek. He had an extraordinary memory, and was a most fluent speaker. He always boasted that to him was owing the establishment of the church at Brunswick, Bangor and Augusta, and also the establishment of the Diocese of Illinois, at a time when there were but two presbyters of the church in the state. At times his enthusiasm amounted to madness. If this had been under better control the good that he would have affected for the church would have been incalculable.

Lowell, all men of high character for talent, integrity, and firmness. Upon leaving college my name was entered as a student in Mr. Lowell's office, though going immediately afterwards to Europe, I never entered it. He was a man of great ability and very ardent temperament, but his nervous irritability was so great that his health would not bear the excitement of his profession, and he retired from it before his 30th year and travelled in Europe. He had great powers of conversation, and as in mixed company he was listened to with attention, he frequently engrossed the attention of the whole audience. He was a warm politician, with strong feelings against Napoleon and the French, from whom he considered the liberties of all the world to be in danger. In those days, when we were dependent upon sailing ships for our news from Europe, we were in the winter generally 60, and sometimes 90, days without information of the great events that were transpiring upon the continent. Upon the arrival of a packet, Lowell would take an elevated position in the Suffolk Insurance Office, and the papers just arrived being handed to him, he would read aloud to a densely crowded room the news, making his comments as he read, which were received as oracular by his eager listeners. He was equally ardent in his religious feelings, and when the theological seminary was established at Andover in order to check the growing tendency to Unitarianism, he put out a pamphlet with the remarkable title, 'Are you a Christian or are you a Calvinist?' A Dutch merchant being here at the time bought it as a curiosity, asking what his good mother would think of it, who did not suppose that anyone could be a Christian who was *not* a Calvinist. Mr. Lowell was a very active member of Harvard College, and introduced many useful reforms in its management, and greatly improved the grounds round the buildings.

Judge Prescott, while his principles were as firm and unbending as those of Mr. Lowell, and their political views harmonized, both being very decided Federalists, differed in all other traits of character from him. Judge Prescott's delight was at the fireside, or with a small circle of friends, when his rich and flowing conversation delivered in mild accents, charmed those friends who loved and admired him.

Judge Parker had neither the ardour of Lowell nor the retired gentleness of Prescott, but his manners were composed and dignified, and the soundness of his legal decisions gave him a high reputation as a judge. He had been taken from the bar to be made Chief Justice, and his brethren on the bench acquiesced in the propriety of his being placed over them. His position as Chief Justice prevented his taking an openly active part in politics.

To counteract the natural indolence of his disposition, he never allowed himself to postpone to the morrow what could be done today. The reports show a very large portion of the judgments of the Supreme Court as coming from his pen, and show how completely he mastered any tendency in his nature to self indulgence. There was a general fear among the most respectable portion of the community of the effect of radical opinions, which were rapidly gaining ground, and which threatened to throw the whole power of the government into the hands of uneducated and unprincipled demagogues, and to endanger the stability of our most valued institutions. Nathan Hale, therefore, editor of the most important paper in Boston, was invited to be a member of the Law Club, in order that, his own political views being enlightened on conservative principles, he might, by means of his paper, influence public opinion in the right direction.

Judge Parker was suddenly taken away by apoplexy in the midst of his usefulness. Though he had lived economically, his salary had been barely sufficient for the support of a large family, and the bar showed their estimate of his worth and services by raising a fund for the support of his widow and children.

To return to my own affairs.

Previously to 1812, I had managed my affairs without any clerical assistance, keeping regular books by double entry, in which I had taken a few lessons from Mr. Sheppard, whom I have previously mentioned. I found, however, the labour too great, and engaged George Shaw, who had been highly recommended to me, as a clerk, and took him into the house, where I fitted up a room for an office, as being more convenient. Shaw was not deficient in intelligence, and when there was a press of business the excitement would enable him to perform it very rapidly and well, but he was heedless and without any fixed principle, and when there was no excitement he would be careless, work would be delayed, and what was accomplished would not be done well.

About the same time that I found it necessary to have a clerk, your mother found that she needed assistance in giving our young children the first rudiments of learning. Miss Amelia Hyde was recommended as a suitable person for that situation and was received into our family as an instructress to our children, the oldest of whom was then under 7 years of age. Miss Hyde's lot in life had been hard, which, while it had stimulated her to great exertion, had not softened her character. Her father had died when she was just coming into life, and had left her and her mother totally destitute. Though young and with little education, she undertook the instruction of a primary school, the emolument of which was only sufficient for the bare support of herself and her mother. Could she obtain a little more instruction herself, she felt that she had the ability to keep a higher school and thus obtain a more comfortable subsistence for herself and her mother. In this laudable endeavour she found friends to assist her. Mrs. Boardman, who kept a school for young ladies, offered to receive her as a pupil without pay. One friend offered her a lodging near the school, and another to pay for her meals. With the money given her for these meals, she supported her mother, allowing herself only two crackers a day and water, hardly enough to sustain the healthy action of the vital organs, and wholly inadequate to allay the cravings of a more than ordinary appetite.

This exertion and filial devotion does her great credit, but there were points in her character which prevented her from being an agreeable inmate. Her temper was jealous and sensitive, and she was always fearful that she should not be treated with sufficient respect. She wished at all times to take a prominent part in the family circle, whether we were alone or had friends staying with us, and showed ill temper if she thought herself neglected. She remained with us two years, but being aware that she was not a favourite in the family, doubtful if she could retain her situation, and dreading being again thrown alone upon the world, she was determined to find a permanent home. She had some connections up in the country, and we consented that Shaw should take her in a chaise we lent them to visit those friends. They were absent three or four days, and on their return we were informed that they were engaged to be married. No match could have been worse assorted, and both probably repented when it was too late. She was the elder by several years, of which he was not aware at the time. Shaw was not industrious and soon fell into idle company, with whom he spent most of his time. Having failed in a little store, his brother in law Swan put him on a farm, where his wife laboured beyond her strength to support the family, and at length sank under it. The children did fairly in the world.

After Miss Hyde left us, we took Moses Springer into our house as an instructor of our children. Springer was naturally a man of considerable ability, and, with very few advantages he had cultivated his own mind and acquired a good deal of knowledge. Your mother was not satisfied with his manners with the children, and he left the house at the end of the year, and I took him into my office. Miss Stone was then our instructress for a few months, and was succeeded in that office by Mr. Titcomb, a simple minded young man from Farmington. He had been brought up in a farmer's family, with only the education of a country academy. He had rarely been from home, and his manners were rustic, but he was a man of principle and exerted himself faithfully to instruct our children, and they were not of an age to require a higher course of training than he was competent to give.

In 1815 we became interested in the account that James Dumaresq gave us of Louisa Lithgow, granddaughter of my Uncle John Gardiner. He said that she was living at

Bath with two aunts in advanced life, one a widow and the other a maiden, in very narrow circumstances. He described her situation as very uncomfortable and in every respect unfavorable, and he was sure that we could not know her without becoming interested in her. His representations induced us to ask her to pass a few days with us. She was handsome, with prepossessing manners, modest, and of great sweetness of disposition. She soon found a way to our hearts, and we told her that she must hereafter consider herself as one of the family and our house as her permanent home, and she was ever after treated as a daughter. Her mind was in a strange state. Her aunts, without being religious, had adopted the received opinions of the extreme Calvinists, and from them Louisa had imbibed the notion that salvation was the free gift of God and would be bestowed on the elect, irrespective of any exertions on their part, and that those who were to be saved would receive the outpourings of the Holy Spirit, which would at once change their dispositions and character. Till that change took place, they might indulge as freely as they chose in all the pleasures of the world without a thought of the future, but when this conversion did take place, the change would be immediate and total, things of the world would lose their interest, and their thoughts and aspirations be absorbed in a future world. Till then, whatever frivolity they chose to indulge in would make no hindrance to their acceptance with God. Without any violent attempt to show the fallacy of these opinions, the silent influence of the family gradually changed these views, and during her residence with us she became an earnest, devoted, and enlightened Christian.

After being with us about four years, she married Edward Williams of Augusta. Though not serious himself, he could not help highly respecting her consistent religious character. Before her marriage there was a tendency to consumption, which in little more than a year brought her to the grave. I passed an hour with her two days before her decease. She was fully aware that the time of her departure was at hand. Her countenance beamed with ecstatic joy, while her beauty was heightened by the hectic flush on her cheek, and, while she spoke of the happy change that awaited her, she seemed filled with love of her Redeemer, and as if she could penetrate through the dark vale of the shadow of death, and see those heavenly mansions open ready to receive her.

*Note of R. H. G. 2nd.

In his "Letters on the Eastern States" Uncle William speaks of a noted character, Mrs. Tom, who lived in a hovel just outside of Oaklands on the road to the village. I can remember her hobbling up to the house so lame as to walk with difficulty, her pail would be well filled with cold meat, etc. and after getting out of sight she would throw away a good part of the provisions and walk off briskly and if she met any one she would speak of the hard-heartedness of the people in the great house who would never give her anything. When she died Griffin was employed to bury her which he did on the flat at the mouth of the Rolling Dam. Griffin occasionally got drunk, and when he did he was in mortal terror, as he said that then the ghost of Mother Tom always chased him as he passed her grave. Speaking of Griffin recalls a remarkable incident. About the year 1824 Griffin was hunting with his gun in the woods just below Rolling Dam when on the south side of a steep hill he suddenly discovered smoke issuing from a tall hollow stump. Approaching it he heard voices under ground, and stepping upon a concealed trap door it gave way, when Griffin gave a fearful leap, and never stopped running till he arrived at Oaklands and announced the fearful news. His story was received with incredulity, but was found to be true. A man and his wife had dug out a square room in a steep hill of clay, and so arranged that a tall stump served as a chimney. The roof was supported by poles, and there was a small hole on the lower side concealed with boughs by which they entered. The screams of terror of Griffin had alarmed the occupants and they fled and were never discovered, but they were supposed to be a couple who had been occasionally seen, and by whom petty pilfering had been committed. In speaking of Mother Tom who lived to the north of Oaklands, another noted character should have been mentioned—Mrs. Francis who lived on the road about as far to the south. She had been a slave in Jamaica. She lived on the little flat south of Francis brook, and her daughters Mrs. Swan, a huge black woman called the Black Swan, and her son Jack Canard lived with her. They were all respectable people, and Jack bought a farm at S. Gardiner and moved the old house down, placing it near his own, and in this his mother lived till her death.

CHAPTER 19

ROBERT HALLOWELL'S LAST DAYS

My father had naturally a strong constitution, and his habits of life were regular. Though not an epicure, he was fond of having on his table the best the market afforded. He disliked French cookery, and the viands on his table were always excellent and plainly but well dressed. He was fond of having one or two friends dine with him, but he had more pleasure in helping them to the tidbits than in eating them himself. Wine in those days was much more freely used than at present, and it added to my father's pleasure to give his friends a glass of choice Madeira. He seldom himself drank more than two or three glasses. He was equally temperate in his eating, saying that he always left the table with his appetite not fully satisfied. Notwithstanding his temperate habits, he began, as he approached his grand climacteric, to be afflicted with gout, the common complaint of the time, and from which both his brothers and sister suffered. Till then he had enjoyed uninterrupted health. Subsequently he had an attack of gout almost every year, which constantly increased in severity and gradually undermined his strong constitution. Towards the close of the winter of 1815-16 he had a severe and protracted illness from which he was not expected to recover. My friend Dr. Gorham attended him and expected for some time that each day would be his last, and attributed his final recovery rather to the extreme weakness of his system, too feeble for disease to take strong hold of, than strength to resist it. Once, when Dr. Gardiner was visiting him, he seemed so near his departure that the Dr. used, from the office for the sick, the commendatory prayer when the spirit seemed about to leave this tenement of clay. The Doctor was remarkable for reading the church service with perfect correctness and in a scholarlike manner, but without

ROBERT HALLOWELL

By Stuart

the unction that would carry it to the hearts of his hearers. But the Doctor was fond of my father, and in this instance he offered the prayer with deep feeling and with an impressiveness which I shall never forget.

My father survived this severe illness, but his mind and body never recovered their former healthy state, and it was evident that he was no longer in a situation to remain alone in the charge of his household, and he readily assented to leave Boston and take up his residence with me in Gardiner. We induced Sally Dodge, who had been a domestic in his family for three and twenty years, to come with him and devote herself entirely to making his remaining years comfortable. He continued to reside with us more than two years. An attack of influenza, which was apparently slight at first, terminated his life after only a few days illness. I was returning from Boston, where I had been a few days without any knowledge that my father was not as well as usual, but a messenger met me in the stage six miles from home to tell me of his dangerous illness, and before I reached the house his spirit had departed. I was not with him to close his eyes, and if I had been, his mind was too far gone to have given me his parting blessing. His constitution had been too much shattered by his severe suffering in Boston to allow him afterwards much enjoyment of life. He was subject to frequent pain, which was sometimes acute, his memory had failed, and his mind frequently wandered. When his friends from Hallowell visited him, he would brighten up, and if their visit did not extend beyond half an hour, they would leave with the impression that he was but little altered, but the excitement never lasted beyond the time, after which his mind relapsed into its wandering state. He would fancy that his room was filled with company who were fatiguing him, and so perfect was the illusion, that he would point his finger to where they were. At the same time his habitual politeness made him desirous that they should not be treated with rudeness, and while he whispered to us his great desire that they should go away, he begged that it might be done so as not to give them offence. He had always entertained a respect for religion, and was gratified when I came forward to openly profess my faith in Christ, but he never partook of the sacrament till his illness in Boston, and never afterwards but in the sick chamber. He was a most kind and indulgent parent, and as I only remained after the loss of his wife and all his other children, he was of course the most strongly attached to me. His fondness was carried to the extent of an unreasonable anxiety. When I had taken your mother to Hallowell, if we did not return as early as he expected, he would walk up and down the bank of the river till he had seen us safely landed from the ferry boat. This anxiety about possible evils, he used to call putting misery out at interest, but, though he thus acknowledged its unreasonableness, he never could subdue it.

My father was large in person and remarkably handsome. His benevolent courtesy gave a pleasing expression to his countenance, and his agreeable manners made him a general favourite in society. Your mother was much struck with his picturesque appearance in his daily trips across the river in his large log canoe, with his favorite terrier seated in the bow, rowing himself with two oars, but not cross handed. A crowd of boys watched his approach to the shore ready to assist in securing the boat, knowing well that there were apples and gingerbread ready to reward them for their trouble.* He was ever administering to the wants of the widow and the fatherless. He wanted three months of being 79 years old at the time of his death in April, 1818. A single slab with the date of his birth and death denotes the places of his sepulture on the south side of Christ Church, Gardiner.

*In speaking of the crowd of boys watching the landing of grandfather knowing the generous supply of gingerbread and apples they would receive, it is not out of the way to say that one of the chief articles of trade to the Byrons and Gays and perhaps the foundation of their fortune was the sale of gingerbread nuts and apples to grandfather who always kept his pockets filled ready for the boys.

TUDOR

Parents	Children
JUDGE WILLIAM TUDOR, youngest son of Deacon John Tudor of Boston 1750-1819 m. Delia Jarvis 1753-1843	WILLIAM TUDOR 1779-1830 unmarried
	JOHN HENRY TUDOR 1782-1802 unmarried
	FREDERIC TUDOR 1783-1864 m. Euphemia Fenno
	EMMA JANE TUDOR 1785-1865 m. Robert Hallowell Gardiner who wrote these memoirs
	DELIA TUDOR 1787-1861 m. Commodore Charles Stewart
	HENRY JAMES TUDOR 1791-1864 m. Fanny H. Foster

CHAPTER 20

JUDGE TUDOR

Your grandfather Tudor, upon graduating at Harvard College in 1769, entered the office of John Adams, the future president of the United States, as a student at law.

The troubles of the revolution had already commenced when he had completed his studies, and all the ardent spirits were attracted from the quiet pursuits of life to the profession of arms.

Gen. Washington's headquarters were at Cambridge, and Mr. Tudor became his private secretary, having been introduced to him by Mr. Adams. He soon after received the appointment of Judge Advocate of the American Army, from which, though unusual, the title of Judge was given to him by which he was afterwards addressed. While stationed at Cambridge, he was in the habit of spending his evenings at Noodles Island with your grandmother, to whom he was then engaged, swimming across Charles River with his clothes upon his head, and returning the same way. He was married before the close of the war and resumed his profession, and though not a profound lawyer, he was eminently successful as a popular advocate. Having an extensive and lucrative practice, many young men who afterwards became highly distinguished were attracted to his office as students. Among them were Fisher Ames, the pure statesman and eloquent orator, Josiah Quincy, who has filled such a great variety of offices with distinction, and the eminent Chief Justice Parker.

Upon the death of his father, the Judge came into possession of a handsome fortune, having as the only son been made the principal heir. He then relinquished his profession and indulged his long cherished wish of travelling in Europe. Mrs. Tudor retired with the children, who were then small, to a farm called Rockwood in the town of Lynn,

JUDGE WILLIAM TUDOR

Artist Unknown

now Saugus, which he had taken for debt, and on which he had built a neat plain house for the residence of Mrs. Tudor's mother and her second husband. Upon his return from Europe, the Judge did not resume his profession. Being fond of the country he varied his life by spending a few weeks at a time at Rockwood.

The Judge had no taste for farming and gave no attention to it; the soil of Rockwood was poor and though great expense was laid out upon it, it yielded little returns. Neither the Judge nor Mrs. Tudor had the least notion of economy. He had spent freely abroad, and she freely at home, and a large sum advanced to William, which was sunk in an unfortunate voyage to Italy, made large inroads upon his property. But the South Boston speculation was the principal cause of the ruin of his fortune.

He was an admirer of the beauties of nature, and in youth was a great walker. One of his favorite rambles was to Dorchester Heights where he would sit and admire the beautiful harbour, with its numerous and diversified islands, and its shipping constantly arriving with rich cargoes from every portion of the globe, and then turning to the town, which seemed cramped into a narrow space, incapable of expansion for its rapidly increasing commerce, the thought occurred to him that if the point at which he stood could be united by a bridge to the old peninsula, space would be given for the increase of the town, and it would be at once covered with streets and houses. The more he meditated upon the scheme, the more feasible it seemed, and he engaged several gentlemen with large capital to engage with him in the plan. The obtaining an Act to annex the peninsula of Dorchester to Boston was accomplished without difficulty, but this went but a small way towards effecting the object. The people of the south part of the town got the impression that a bridge built where proposed would materially lessen the value of their property, and were deaf to all arguments in its favour and all terms of compromise, the Proprietors of South Boston having offered to pay to every vessel passing the bridge ample compensation for the delay the bridge would cause. Mr.

Otis, one of the speculators, made a most powerful argument in favour of the project, but in vain. The contest was carried on for several years, when a compromise was effected, the Company consenting to locate their bridge beyond the existing wharves, and to connect it with the business part of the town by a street passing over the head of those wharves. Large expenditures were then made to prepare the lands for building purposes. Hills had to be leveled, marshes to be raised, streets to be made and graded. For these purposes heavy assessments were laid on the property, to meet which the Judge was obliged to make loans sometimes at high rates of interest, and to give such security as he was able. But notwithstanding these expenditures, the land had no marketable value till after many years a bridge was built where first proposed, which realized the expectation of the projectors, but the Judge's shares had previously passed out of his hands.

The year after our marriage, the Judge's income having become inadequate to meet the current family expenses, Mrs. Tudor proposed the desperate remedy of breaking up housekeeping, selling their furniture and books, and with the proceeds going to Europe, leaving Frederic to raise from the remnants of the property what further might be needed to pay expenses.

The Judge did not readily assent to the plan, but though hasty and even violent in opposing what did not please him, yet he was very placable, and his indolent temperament made him, after the first ebullition had passed, readily yield to the influence of your grandmother, who was always sure by perseverance and allowing the first excitement to pass off without opposition eventually to obtain what she wished. In the autumn they sailed for England and thence went for a time to Paris.

Your grandfather could speak no language but his native tongue, and having no decided literary or scientific taste to make his society courted and having previously made what was then called the grand tour of Europe, was very glad to get back to the place of his nativity and the friends of his earlier and more mature years. He left your grandmother and aunt Delia in England.

Upon your grandfather Tudor's return from Europe, he was elected to the office of Secretary of State, although he had never been an active partisan, and parties at that time were much embittered against each other. But he had a warmth and cordiality that made him active friends, by whose exertions he obtained the office. The salary was moderate, but the place was exactly suited to his taste. He had a large office handsomely furnished, and supplied with all the newspapers of the day, while the drudgery was performed by clerks long familiar with the duties, and requiring but slight superintendence. His principal duties were to keep the records of the Council when in session, and to carry messages from the Governor to either branch of the Legislature, which he did with some parade, dressed in his velvet coat and preceded by a messenger, with his staff of office, to announce his coming. In 1811, when the Democratic party came into power, although your grandfather was on friendly terms with many of its leaders, who would have retained him in office, there were too many hungry applicants for his place, and he was removed in order to reward active partisans.

Your grandmother remained in Europe a year or two after your grandfather, and upon her return they rented a small house in Belknap Street behind the State House, which Mrs. Tudor furnished with great taste, considering her limited means.

Judge Parker, who was cousin to Mrs. Tudor, appointed the Judge Clerk of the Supreme Court, an office very much less to his taste than his former one. The emolument was much greater, but the duties were labourious and irksome, and the responsibilities great. He had never been in the habit of keeping accounts and was always careless of money, and at the end of three or four years he was unable to account for all the fees that had passed through his hands. Mr. Quincy was on his bond and was much excited, but I cheerfully stept into the gap, and paid the deficiency, which did not amount to $1000. The Judge put into my hands as security property which eventually was worth more than what I had paid, and which I made over to Mrs. Tudor as collected.

Your grandfather Tudor died in 1819. Lameness from

the bad setting of a broken leg had deprived him of the pleasure of rambling in the country and admiring the beauties of nature, of which he was so fond, and the drudgery of the Clerk's office had latterly become irksome to him, but he never complained of these changes of fortune, but retained his cheerfulness to the last, and was ever alive to the growing prosperity of his native city which he had always been fond of promoting, and on which he loved to expatiate. He was a member of most of the societies for the benefit of its citizens, and of several, their presiding officer.

He made us an annual visit of a week or ten days every summer and showed an interest in all the improvements that were going forward. He had ever entertained a strong desire that when the time of his departure out of this life should arrive, he should be taken away without any previous lingering sickness, and this wish was fully gratified. After a slight indisposition, he awoke early one morning and begged your grandmother to open the shutters that he might once more see the light of the glorious sun. This wish being gratified, he fell back and expired without a groan, at the age of 70.

Upon the death of your grandfather Tudor, your grandmother came to make this her home, and she made a very agreeable addition to our large family circle. Her mode of life with us was contrary to all the received rules for the preservation of health. She rose late and breakfasted in her chamber, and never came downstairs till near dinner time, when she ate very heartily, and never went out of the house from October to April except riding to church once on Sunday. She kept her mind constantly active, which she said preserved the body in health as well as exercise. When indisposed, which was rare, living a couple of days on gruel restored her exhausted powers to their natural vigour. She made herself particularly agreeable to the young members of the family, who were all very fond of her. There was one peculiar trait in your grandmother of which I have never known another instance. When anything distressing occurred, she was overwhelmed with it till she could unburthen herself to some one whose sympathies she could command. To your mother these outpourings were overwhelming. I therefore became the object of them, and I was glad that I could thus relieve your mother. Till your grandmother had thus relieved herself, her distress was great, but as soon as she had apparently placed the burden upon the shoulders of some one else, her usual serenity returned, and it would seem as if her trouble was forgotten. She remained an inmate of our family for more than seven years, till the final breach between Mrs. Stewart and the Commodore.

Your grandfather Tudor in his embarrassment had borrowed of Parkman monies at usurious interest, and had given him security on the Court St. house. Your uncle Frederic thought he could make Parkman disgorge this usurious interest, and he proposed to the heirs that if they would relinquish to him all their interest in the property, he would allow your grandmother an annuity of $500. This was readily assented to, as none of the other heirs were disposed to enter into a lawsuit to contest Parkman's claim upon the property. Parkman was glad to compromise with your uncle, who thus became possessed of the valuable property in Court So. for a very moderate sum.

Your grandmother proposed that she should appropriate this annuity, with additions from other members of the family to a summer residence at Nahant. None of the children did contribute, and your uncle paid all the bills for the house and owns the property*. While your grandmother was with us, her annuity went towards it, but after she left us and joined Mrs. Stewart at Washington where they kept house, it became necessary for her own support.

*Note of R. H. G. 2nd.

When grandmother proposed that all the family should unite in building a cheap cottage at Nahant, where she should pass the summer, and the different members of the family visit in turn, the house was framed here and with all the materials shipped directly to Nahant. Mr. Tudor took charge of its erection, and added so much to its proposed cost, that by general consent the house was relinquished to him.

CHAPTER 21

OTHER TUDOR RELATIONS

When the family broke up, your uncle Harry (Henry Tudor) was at school at Dr. Gardiner's, preparatory to his entering Harvard at the next Commencement. His college vacations were spent with us at Gardiner. He was at an age when impressions are made that become permanent through life. Your mother obtained a very beneficial influence over him, and if the habits he was then forming had not been interrupted, they would with his fine powers of mind have made him a distinguished man. But your uncle Frederic counteracted this influence by ridiculing him for being under petticoat government, and what youth can withstand that taunt? Several of his next years were wasted in idleness.

It was about this time that the Emperor Napoleon, bent upon the destruction of England as the only obstacle to his obtaining universal dominion, issued his decrees against the commerce and manufactures of Great Britain.

Stephen Higginson, Jr., a gentleman of ample fortune, but with more zeal than judgment, and with strong anti-Gallican feelings, formed a scheme for counteracting the decrees, benefiting England, and acquiring great wealth for himself, as if his puny efforts could impede the iron will of the despot against whose course not a government on the continent dared even to protest. Wilder had been already sent to disregard the paper blockades and to flood Holland and Germany with English manufactures, and your uncle William was sent to assist him. It is scarcely necessary to say that Higginson did not cause the downfall of Napoleon, but that he did bring utter ruin upon himself. Upon Higginson's failure your uncle engaged with some American gentlemen in setting up the manufacture of nails under the patent of Jacob Perkins. Your uncle had the

WILLIAM TUDOR, JR.

Portrait at Oaklands—by Stuart

agency, but he was not successful in overcoming the prejudices against cut nails and in favour of those wrought by hand. The manufacture was abandoned, and your uncle returned to this country. In 1811, after the failure of the nail factory at Birmingham, he spent a year with us at Oaklands. His bonhomie and playful wit made him a delightful companion. He was full of the milk of human kindness, and had the warmest affection for your mother and our children. He had good taste, was fond of the fine arts, was patriotic and public spirited, and if he had been blessed with fortune would have made himself a useful member of society, as well as being its ornament, but he was wholly deficient in business capacity, and knew not how to live with small means. During the winter, with the cat on his arm for a companion he wrote a pleasing work, "Letters on the Eastern States." At the same time he was devising some scheme to give him an independent support.

The anti-commercial scheme devised by Mr. Jefferson and followed by his successor till northern shipping was driven from the ocean, drove the New Englanders, living in a cold climate and on a barren soil, to seek other occupations, and they at once turned their attention to manufactures. The water power on our larger rivers was not then known to be available for such purposes, and all the small streams were taken up for the object. Your uncle was familiar with the country round Boston, and there was a pond in Malden much elevated above the surrounding country which he thought, by digging a channel through a narrow embankment, might be made into a valuable mill power. This he obtained the control of, and with the assistance of his friends completed the canal and made the pond discharge into the plain below, but he had not a practical mind, and could not impress upon others his views with sufficient force to induce them to embark in the undertaking and carry into use the power which he had created. Satisfied with seeing the water run as he wished he allowed the property to revert to the mortgagee, its original proprietor. Not long afterwards he obtained through the influence of John Quincy Adams the appointment of Consul to Lima, and the absence of the Minister occurring, he acted for some time as Charge d'affaires, his conduct in which capacity having given satisfaction to the administration, Mr. Clay, Secretary of State at the time, after writing him a complimentary letter, promoted him to the office of Charge d'affaires to the Court of Brazil.

Soon after our marriage, the thought of supplying the West Indies with ice had occurred to him, and was spoken of in the family circle, but whether as a vague passing thought or an enterprise to be entered upon, I do not know, but whichever it might have been, he was wholly deficient in the administrative talent and the energy and perseverance necessary to carry into successful operation any new scheme, however promising*.

The suggestion was not lost upon his brother Frederic, who after deliberating upon it, determined to carry it into operation. The difficulties attending it were much greater than were anticipated. The idea was considered so utterly absurd by the sober minded merchants as to be the vagary of a disordered brain, and few men would have been willing to stand the scoffs and sneers from those whose assistance it was necessary to obtain, to aid him in the enterprise. The difficulties attending it were not foreseen, and it required all your uncle's energy and indomitable perseverance, continued through a dozen or more years of disappointment, before he reaped any success. He had no capital and less credit with which to undertake the business. Merchants were not willing to charter their vessels to carry ice. The offices declined to insure, and sailors were afraid to trust themselves with such a cargo. William would have a share in the concern and he and James Savage went out to visit the various West India islands, propose the scheme and obtain privileges for its introduction. Our relations with Spain were such at the time that they did not visit Cuba. Frederic himself followed, with the first cargo to Marti-

*Note of R. H. G. 2nd.

The reasons alluded to, but not given, why Mr. Tudor gave up the experiment of procuring ice from the Kennebec was first the great amount of sawdust in the ice. Next the tides which compelled the changing of his hoisting apparatus every hour, third, the great amount of snow, the idea of scraping not then having been thought of, and, lastly, the difficulty of obtaining freights.

nique, some weeks afterwards. The necessity of an ice house had not been thought of, nor was he aware of the prejudice of the people against its use, and the time it would require to teach the public its value as a most grateful luxury, or its aid to the physician in administering to his patients in the attacks of fever peculiarly virulent in tropical climates. He eventually overcame the prejudices and succeeded in establishing the ice business in several of the West India islands, but it was not till he supplied the thriving and luxurious city of Havana with what they soon learnt to be a first necessary of life that he began to reap a golden harvest, and to show in a striking manner the fallacy of the old notion of the balance of the trade, the principle of which was that a country must be carrying on a losing business when the value of imports exceeded that of the exports. Here Mr. Tudor exchanged a cargo of ice of almost nominal value, for a cargo of sugar or molasses. He subsequently established his ice business at New Orleans, but as he was still without the requisite capital, it was only through the various great personal exertions of your uncle Harry in obtaining there the means of erecting the ice house that he was successful.

The ice business is now one of the most profitable branches of business carried on in Boston, and is extended to all parts of the world. Your uncle was the first bold adventurer to carry ice twice across the equator, and deliver it with the fruits of the northern climates in the heated plains of India. The great profits of the ice business enable him to sustain a loss of between $200,000. and $300,000. from speculating in coffee, to live very expensively, and accumulate a large fortune.

In the early part of 1820, I was notified that your uncle Frederic was taken ill with a severe attack of fever, and as none of his family were then in Boston, I immediately went up to him. He had boarded for many years with Betsey LeKane, and recently had hired and furnished a house in Pearl St. adjoining Betsey's, where he still took his meals. I found him under the professional care of my friend Dr. Jackson, who deemed him very ill, and though he had a regular nurse, the Dr. considered it important that I should remain and take charge of him till he recovered. As he required constant watching, I told the nurse that she might go to bed every night between 8 and 9, and I would take charge of him till 2 or 3 in the morning, when I would call her and go to bed myself. This I did through his illness, and also the frequent rubbing prescribed by the doctor. I sat with him also during the day, except when I took a short walk to get the fresh air. When your uncle became convalescent, your mother came up to see him, and as the doctor said that freedom from all care and anxiety was essential to his recovery, she proposed that he should take a journey and leave the entire charge of his ice concerns, which were then almost his sole business, to my management. When your mother made the proposal, he said in his droll manner, 'What a fool you must be to make yourself my drudge, and allow me to go off to take my ease and recreation.' He, however, consented to the arrangement and went away leaving me with the general superintendence, though he had capable men to take charge of the details. I had to make all the pecuniary arrangements, and for this purpose had to supply considerable funds from my own resources, which were long unpaid, and on which I never charged any interest, or took any compensation for my services. When he returned and resumed the charge of his business, I still continued to give him the benefit of my credit by endorsing his paper in Boston and by raising money for him here. Ice had been put up from here, but from a variety of circumstances, but more particularly the greater facility of shipping it from Boston, he found it more advantageous to have his ice shipped from there. Two winters were so mild that ice could not be procured in Boston, and your uncle sent his foreman, Wyeth, to put up large quantities here. A number of temporary ice houses were erected, some on the high part of my wharf, supposed to be above any common freshet, and a large one on the bank of the river in front of Oaklands, where the water was supposed never to have come. Both winters were followed by spring freshets of unusual height, which reached the ice houses. The current gradually wore away the lower tiers of ice, when the weight of the superincumbent mass, having lost its support, toppled over and carried the whole mass into the river with the temporary structure in which it was piled.

CHAPTER 22

DELIA TUDOR STEWART

Your aunt Delia Tudor was imbued with a most remarkable energy of character and she possessed a perseverance which no difficulties could check. She had a large frame, and her motions were naturally neither easy nor graceful, but by long and unwearied exertions, she acquired the power of moving and dancing with grace and elegance. The same determination for excellence had enabled her to acquire great power both with the harp and piano.* Her music was more artistic than your mother's, but not so full of expression. She had learnt the same lessons under Dr. Gardiner's tuition as the boys in his school, and had acquired sufficient knowledge of Latin to read the poets with ease and pleasure. She had acquired some knowledge of German, and spoke French, Spanish and Italian with fluency. Your grandmother's house was the resort of all foreigners who had any pretensions to be received into society, and as it was then difficult to obtain regular instruction in any foreign language excepting French, your aunt called upon all these visitors to assist her in her studies. Your aunt was near sighted, which injured her expression, but her accomplishments gave her an easy introduction to the first circles both in France and England, at whose courts she was deemed a very fine woman, and her society was sought by many persons of wealth and position.

When your Aunt Delia was in England, staying with various aristocratic families, her company was courted, but in this society besides an expensive wardrobe, many inci-

*Note of R. H. G. 2nd.
In speaking of Aunt Delia's accomplishments, mother used to tell us that her figure and gait were very awkward and that for hours she would daily practise deportment before a long mirror. With little idea of time she became a most graceful dancer, regulating her movements by that of others, although she was near sighted. I remember as a child once asking her to play on the piano; she declined saying that once she was reputed the finest performer in the country, but being no longer so, she should never play again.

dental expenses were necessary, and your uncle Frederic wrote to her that it was impossible for him to remit what she required, and that she must return home forthwith. She delayed as long as possible, but was at length obliged to relinquish the fashionable society where she was accustomed to shine, and in which she so much delighted. It was a severe trial to her to be obliged to exchange the splendid and luxurious apartments of the English metropolis for the dismal contracted rooms of Belknap Street, too small to allow a dozen people to be seated. She was at first received with great attention by the old friends of the family, but she could not forget the contrast between her present and former residences, and content herself with the very narrow mode of living that her parents had been obliged to adopt. Discontented herself, she made the whole household uncomfortable. Your uncle told her that it had become too intolerable to be longer borne, and that, as the only way in which things could be changed, she must consent to be married. Samuel Welles, a respectable gentleman, with ample fortune, had pressed his suit with great earnestness, but he was neither accomplished nor literary, and for some peculiarity of manner had been an object of ridicule to the young ladies of Boston. His suit therefore had been rejected.

Commodore Stewart at this time arrived in Boston in command of the Frigate Constitution. Like most of the naval officers of that day, he had been bred to the sea in the merchant service. His manners were coarse and unpolished, though probably not more so than Lord Nelson's, whom he was said to resemble in person. He was introduced to your aunt as a very able and gallant officer, holding high rank in the service, as a man of more than common ability, and at the same time very rich. She knew the naval officers in England, notwithstanding a little roughness of the sailor, took high positions in society; still she felt a repugnance to Stewart which made her show that she could not accept the hand about to be proffered, and Stewart discontinued his visits. Your uncle could see no other prospect of a marriage for his sister, and he determined that this should not be abandoned. He represented to her Stewart's great wealth, his reputed liberality and generosity, his station in society, nearly at the head of his profession, and at length obtained her consent that he should be again invited to the house. The engagement soon followed, and the consummation was so pressed that we only heard of the engagement the day before the wedding, which had been professedly hastened because of his expected immediate departure on a cruise, though he remained in port a couple of months afterwards.

The wedding took place at Trinity Church on Thanksgiving Day, immediately after the morning service, when the church was filled to suffocation. We were coming up to spend the winter, and arrived the day subsequently. Never was a match more ill assorted. Stewart, possessed of great nautical skill, showed great judgment and determination in command, but he was sensual, fond of gaming and of convivial company, retaining the feelings of the forecastle from which he had been elevated, and neither knowing nor caring anything for the accomplishments of polished life.

Your aunt, with a cold temperament and indifferent to the pleasures of the table, placed her happiness in shining in society, which she was enabled to do by the grace of her manners, her numerous accomplishments, and her acquaintance with the language and literature of the most polished nations in Europe. With tastes and views so incompatible it was impossible that harmony should long exist, and Stewart told me that they quarreled the first night of their marriage, and the more they became acquainted, the more distasteful they became to each other. Stewart remained ashore for several weeks after his marriage, though his officers complained that he should have been at sea cruising for the enemy.

After a short cruise he returned, having captured two British sloops of war, one of which he destroyed and the other he brought into Boston. This added greatly to his eclat, and of course very much to the gratification of your aunt.

In February 1815, on the ratification of peace with Great Britain, your aunt went to live on an extensive and valuable place he owned at Bordentown on the left bank of the Delaware, a few miles below Trenton. He was soon after ordered to cruise in the Mediterranean. He left his wife at Bordentown, but not with sufficient income for the support of herself and children, and she turned into money everything on the farm for which she could find a purchaser, to supply her wants. This dilapidation greatly increased the ill feeling of the Commodore after his return. During his absence she had found the solitude of Bordentown intolerable, and during the two or three years that the cruise lasted she made us several visits, but our quiet mode of living was not to her taste, and she would become restless, rush up to Boston without an object, and then back again. Her excessive love of admiration made her uneasy, except in society. Fond of flattery which could not be too gross to be acceptable, she constantly invited it by the excessive flattery she bestowed upon others. Your uncle Harry accompanied Stewart to the Mediterranean in the nominal office of secretary, which afforded him a fine opportunity of visiting the classical remains of Rome and Italy, and paying short visits to the capitals of England and France. After Stewart's return, your aunt joined him at Bordentown.

In the year 1822, Commodore Stewart was ordered to take command of a small squadron and proceed to the Pacific on a three years' cruise. Mrs. Stewart was invited to accompany him, for the Commodore was not satisfied with her management of the farm at Bordentown which he left in her charge when he was absent on his former cruise in the Mediterranean. On their voyage they stopped at Rio de Janeiro, where Mrs. Stewart was received by the Court with the greatest distinction, not only from the station of her husband, but from her own accomplishments. Her graceful manners, and the fluency with which she spoke both Spanish and Portuguese, excited the greatest admiration. Mrs. Stewart was much surprised, when presented at Court, at meeting negro officers in full uniform holding positions of equality with the whites, so abhorrent to the notions prevalent in the United States as to the coloured races. De Tocqueville observed that the prejudice which existed in the Anglo Saxons against amalgamation with an inferior race did not exist among those of Latin origin. The consequence of this prejudice he thought would be that when the emancipation of the slaves took place, which sooner or later it must do, they would be drawn south from the United States, possibly to form negro governments in the West Indies. We know too little of Brazil to form any correct opinion of what the effect of amalgamation of the three distinct races inhabiting that country will hereafter be. When the squadron arrived in the Pacific, the various republics were in the same state of chronic revolution and rebellion that they had been in for years, and which still continues.

Connected with these political convulsions occurred a circumstance which had a most disastrous influence upon your aunt's fate. The President of Peru had been just defeated, deposed, branded as a traitor, and a large reward offered for his apprehension. He escaped on board the Commodore's ship and threw himself upon your aunt's protection. Her lively imagination at once converted the suppliant into a hero of romance, fleeing from the vindictiveness of a hard-hearted usurper. Her feelings, always alive to those in distress, did not allow her to turn a deaf ear to his petition. She gave him in charge of the steward, who disguised him as one of his assistants, not reflecting that she thereby compromised the character and official position of her husband. The transaction was most carefully concealed from the Commodore, and the fugitive remained on board while the ship was at Callao, and till she reached a point of the coast whence he might make his escape. A demand from the victorious party for the surrender of the deposed president was the first knowledge that Stewart had of the affair. He did not then believe it, and had no hesitation in giving his word of honour that no such person was, or ever had been, on board his ship. The real truth soon came to the knowledge of the Commodore. He felt that his professional reputation was put in jeopardy, that the complaints of the ruling powers in Peru would subject him to be tried by a court-martial by whom he might be dismissed the navy with disgrace, or unpleasant complications might be produced between the new republic and his own country. His rage against his wife became unbounded, and he adopted a most original mode of showing it. He determined never to open his lips again to her during the remainder of the voyage, but she was compelled to take her usual seat at table without the least notice from her husband, and, difficult as it is to understand, no change was made during the long voyage from the Pacific to New York.

No sooner had the ship's anchor been cast in the harbour, than the Commodore seemed to forget the events of the past few months. He waited upon his wife ashore, and during the next few days they called together upon their numerous acquaintances. As soon as the squadron was paid off, Stewart was called to Washington, and his wife came here with her children. He wrote to her from Washington, evidently in great anxiety, that he was to be tried by court-martial for offences of which she was really the guilty person. We were very desirous that she should at once go on to him, but she was like a timid animal in presence of a powerful foe ready to devour it, against whom it has no power of resistance, and whom fear has deprived even of the power of flight. Dread even prevented her from making any reply, and as the court-martial was from various causes protracted thro' the summer into the autumn, she continued here in a most distracted state of mind, which neither our attentions nor the doting sympathy of your grandmother could alleviate. In her restless state she would suddenly go off to Boston or to Newport, as if endeavoring to escape the impending calamity, but the dread still pursued her, and she would as suddenly return. All his urgent appeals to her for explanations of particular circumstances that had occurred in the affair were unanswered, and she only knew the result of the trial, and that the Commodore's sword had been restored to him, by the announcement in the public papers. Your aunt now became alive to her real position, and that she must return to her own home with her children to meet the dreaded wrath of her husband which she had done so much to provoke. She could not think of braving it alone, and she therefore wrote to her friend Mrs. Bright, who was intimately acquainted with the Commodore, to be at Bordentown when she came on, and to assist her in bearing the first ebullition of her husband's rage.

Mrs. Bright was a widow lady of fortune, residing at Elizabethtown, New Jersey. She was very lively and agreeable in conversation, fond of innocent intrigue, and as she had conceived a strong dislike to the Commodore, was quite ready to assist in screening your aunt from his wrath, and to exercise her ingenuity with devising means for his annoyance. Mrs. Bright therefore went at once to the Commodore's house at Bordentown to meet Mrs. Stewart on her arrival. The Commodore was not then residing in his own house but with a Mr. Field about a mile below, with whose wife he was supposed to have tender relations. As soon as he heard of your aunt's arrival, he immediately sent an order for her to quit the house, as he would never consent to again sleep under the same roof with her. She immediately wrote to your uncle Frederic in the most earnest manner to come on to her protection. This letter he inclosed to me, saying that it was impossible for him to go on, and that I was a much more suitable person to manage the business than himself. This letter was received on the evening of Christmas, when, as you well recollect, we were in the habit of assembling all the family connexion, and the evening was devoted to the amusement of the younger members of the party.

These Christmas parties were always successful and in order not to disturb the hilarity of the occasion, the contents of the letter were only communicated that evening to your mother and grandmother. It did seem barbarous that your aunt should be turned out into the street, without any member of her family going on for her protection. I therefore readily acceded to the earnest wishes of your mother and grandmother, and the next day was on my way to Bordentown. I travelled as fast as could be done in those days of slow locomotion, and found your aunt and Mrs. Bright in possession of the Commodore's house and with no disposition to yield possession of it. Mrs. Bright was not a judicious adviser. She took no general view of Mrs.

Stewart's situation, but, as her friend, was bound to resent what she deemed her husband's ill treatment, by giving to him every possible annoyance. My object was conciliation, and as first step I insisted that the Commodore's house, to which he had a perfect right, should be given up to him. It could not indeed have been retained, unless Mrs. Bright or myself would have paid all the expenses of the establishment, for Mrs. Stewart had neither money nor credit. I therefore engaged lodgings at a Mrs. Lippincott's in the village, Mrs. Bright and myself paying our own board, and Mrs. L. looking to the Commodore to pay the expenses of the rest of the party. Mrs. B. disliked the arrangement, as it deprived her of much of her power of annoying the Commodore, and she was obliged to confine herself to listening to the village scandal respecting him. Before seeing the Commodore, it was necessary for me to ascertain your aunt's views and wishes. She told me that she would upon no consideration consent to a separation, that there was something dreadful to her in the name of divorce, and that she would prefer being shut up in a chamber during the remainder of her life than to consent to a legal separation. I found the Commodore equally determined against a reconciliation and that he would never consent to hear a word upon the subject. He then referred me to his counsel, Mr. Hopkinson of Philadelphia, and offered to drive me down in his gig. When we got to Camden opposite to the city, the river was full of floating ice, the wind cold and piercing, and we were a long time in getting over, and upon my return to Bordentown I was laid up with a severe attack of influenza.

Hopkinson had all the acuteness for which Philadelphia lawyers are proverbial, was not scrupulous, but thought everything right which would promote the interest of his client. His father was one of the signers of the Declaration of Independence and resided at Bordentown, which had become a favorite retreat for many Philadelphians during the hot summer weather. Mrs. H. was then the leader of society, but the superior grace and accomplishments of your aunt threw her into the shade, and jealousy produced hostility. The husband, taking up the Commodore's interest against his wife, allowed his feelings to be influenced by his own wife, and he was therefore disposed to regard all Mrs. Stewart's imprudencies in the most unfavorable light. In my first interview with him I was obliged to bring forward the proposition for reconciliation which he said could not be thought of for a moment, and which seemed to me not in the least desirable, for Stewart told me that he and his wife quarreled the first night of their marriage, and after the exasperation which had since taken place, if harmony could be restored, it was not probable that it would last 24 hours. Hopkinson's proposition was that a legal separation between the parties should be made, that Mrs. Stewart should give up to the Commodore all control of the children, that he should allow her $800. per annum, and receive ample security against any of his wife's present or future debts. I at once replied that I would communicate the proposals to Mrs. Stewart, but should advise her that they were such as she ought not to agree to, that she was devotedly attached to her children who reciprocated her affection, that the Commodore's allowance when he was absent in the Mediterranean not being adequate to her support, she had been obliged to borrow monies which must be repaid, and that the proposed alimony was not in proportion to his fortune, or adequate to support her in the style of living to which she had been accustomed. Mrs. Stewart was of course very indignant at these proposals when I communicated them to her. I told her that he had one of the most acute and unscrupulous lawyers in Philadelphia opposed to us, that I wished to have legal advice also, and suggested Mr. Meredith with whom I was intimately acquainted. I knew him to be a man of the kindest and most honourable feelings, and one who had a respectable standing at the bar; and with her assent I went down to Philadelphia to consult him. Arriving late in the evening I delayed my visit to Mr. M. till the next morning, when, to my utter surprise, I found that Mrs. Stewart had travelled all night and had got to Mr. M's house before me. This was evidence that altho' she had accepted me as her friend and protector, she did not give me that confidence to which one in my situation was entitled. She was aware that there was much in her conduct which I did not approve, and she feared lest I should let Hopkinson [Meredith?] know of that disapprobation. I had drawn up a counter project, which I showed to Mr. Meredith, and which with a slight modification he approved. I demanded that Mrs. Stewart should have the entire control of one of the children, that her debts should be paid and that she should have a larger alimony. When this was refused, I told your aunt that there were but two courses to be pursued—to accept such terms, however disadvantageous, as could be procured, or to sue for her rights in a court of law, and I had intimated to Hopkinson that such would probably be the course to which we should be driven. He replied that he had in his possession such evidence as would prevent any court from allowing her more than nominal alimony, and should prove that she was not a suitable person to have charge of her minor children. He then explained, 'She has borrowed money of Count Serveilliers (Joseph Bonaparte) and you know,' he added, 'what is the understanding when a married woman borrows money of a single gentleman without the knowledge of her husband.' He said also that he had evidence that she had gone late in the evening to a house of ill-fame. I replied to Hopkinson that, as Stewart himself had not suspected his wife of infidelity, for he added that her constitution was so cold that she had no temptation, he could not believe in such grossness. He only repeated that if a suit was commenced in court he should certainly bring forward the evidence he had referred to and which could not be rebutted. When I stated this conversation to your aunt, she utterly denied that she had ever borrowed money of the Count, and explained her going to a bad house by saying that she did not know its character, which was doubtless true, and that feeling anxious about her situation she had gone there to have her fortune told by a woman who had acquired a great reputation in being able to pry into the future. When I told Hopkinson that your aunt gave me the most solemn assurances that she had never borrowed money of the Count, he gave me a most peculiar and sarcastic look, as much as to say "Are you such a simpleton as to be so easily deceived? My authority is the

Count himself who related to me all the circumstances." Mrs. Stewart's subsequent reply to me was, "Did you think me such a fool that I would criminate myself?" Under all these circumstances it seemed to me that I could no longer be of any use. Having by further negotiation obtained some relaxation from Hopkinson, he having agreed that Mrs. Stewart should have the entire control and management of one of the children and that the Commodore should pay all the debts of which Mrs. Stewart had rendered a schedule, I told her that if she had made up her mind that she would not agree to these terms, nor would consent to a suit for separation, that there was no use in my remaining longer and that I must return home. When she found that I was to leave she became almost distracted among the children, lest they should be taken from her at once, and urged me to take them with me. This I declined, as interfering with their father's rights. I most sincerely pitied her situation. It was impossible for parties with views and tastes and opinions so entirely opposed as those of the Commodore and his wife to have the mutual affection necessary for the happiness of the married state, yet I was conscious that the evils had been greatly aggravated by her course of conduct. Still I was anxious to alleviate her sufferings, and consented that she should send on the children with their nurse to my house and furnished her with the means to pay their expenses. On the 10th of February I left for home, having spent seven weeks most uncomfortably and without effecting the object for which I had come. The journey was not however without its benefit to Mrs. S. The Commodore was disappointed at finding that he could not throw her off without her having friends to come forward for her protection and that he was obliged to offer terms which, though not as liberal as they ought to have been, were not such as would injure her standing in the community. When I got home I found the children had arrived the day before me, and Mrs. Stewart came shortly after. In a few days I received a letter from Hopkinson charging me with the offence of abducting the children and secreting them from their father. I immediately replied that the children were in my house, where they would remain till their father chose to send for them, for which I claimed no right to keep them. Your aunt had an agony of grief and terror at my letter, and was devising a thousand schemes to conceal the children should their father send for them, but Hopkinson told Stewart that the children would not be so well off as where they were if I had not children enough of my own and was disposed to keep them. Charles remained with us about two years when, your mother finding our family inconveniently large, I wrote to the Commodore and he immediately sent on his nephew, Lieut. McCauley, and he took Charles away. While with us he had a severe fever. Upon his recovery I sent the physician's bill and also a bill for the boy's clothes on for payment, but Hopkinson wrote in reply that the Commodore declined paying any bills for the children while they were with me. Delia remained nearly a year longer, when Mrs. Stewart finally acceded to the terms offered her before I left Bordentown. The schedule of her debts handed in contained only the smaller part of what she owed, for her natural timidity prevented her from stating the whole truth at once, but they would allow nothing to be added to the schedule, and the other debtors were left unpaid. Delia was to remain with her mother and Charles with his father, and I signed the tripartite agreement by which I became bound to hold the Commodore harmless from any future debts of his wife, and he became bound to pay my quarterly order in her favour of $200. This was done for my security, as when a bill was sent to the Commodore against his wife he forwarded it to me, and I stopped the amount out of the next quarter's payment.

Some years afterwards President Polk visited Maine, and Commodore Stewart came in his suite. Mr. Evans and some other gentlemen of the place were desirous that some attention should be shown by Gardiner to the President. I therefore went to Augusta and called at Mr. Williams' on the President and his party, whom I invited to my house. To the Commodore I gave a special and particular invitation. The party came in a steamer from Augusta to Gardiner, and thence to my house in carriages.* The Commodore however felt the offence so deeply of my having protected his wife from his rage and taken care of his children for several years, that he did not choose to come down with the rest of the party but remained on the wharf during the hour they remained with us. Such was the close of my intercourse with Commodore Stewart.

When the papers of separation were finally signed, your grandmother, who had resided with us since the death of your grandfather left us to reside at Washington with your aunt. To your aunt's $800 per annum she added the $500. which your uncle Frederic stipulated to pay her on the relinquishment to him of the interest the heirs had in the Court St. house, and your aunt interested J. Q. Adams, who had studied law with your grandfather to exert himself in their favour, and he got an Act thro' Congress allowing the heirs of your uncle the salary of Charge d'Affaires when he acted in that capacity in Lima. The amount was between $4000. and $5000., which the heirs and creditors relinquished to your grandmother.

*Note of R. H. G. 2nd.
The President and his party coming from Augusta in steamer is a mistake. They came in barouches, a cavalcade from Augusta and Hallowell escorting them to the Gardiner line; there they were met by an escort on horseback from Gardiner, who conducted them to Oaklands, the steamer New England meanwhile awaiting them at the Freight Station. It was a dusty time, and so many horsemen raised a fearful amount of dust, so that it was impossible to distinguish one person from another. The President on his arrival was immediately conducted into father's room and furnished with the means of a thorough ablution, for which he expressed the warmest gratitude. Mr. Buchanan and other members of the Cabinet and Judge Clifford were of the party. After a rest of an hour and refreshments, the party returned to the steamboat. An immense crowd was gathered upon the wharf, and Mr. Evans made one of his happiest and most eloquent speeches, the President in his reply saying that nothing in his whole tour had equalled it or affected him so much.

CHAPTER 23

BUSINESS AGENTS

In 1815 Moody Noyes from Newburyport called upon me and earnestly intreated me to give him employment. He had been in the class before me in college, where I had slightly known him. He was a classmate of your uncle John [Tudor], and his warm admiration of your uncle had made the family interested in him, but he was one of those unfortunate persons to whom education, by raising him from the sphere in which he had been brought up to a station for which his talents were unequal, had been a disservice. Without the acquirements or ability necessary to succeed in a profession, he had learnt to look contemptuously on mechanical employments, and knew not how to support himself. During a long winter vacation, in the early part of his college course, a religious revival took place in his native town of Newburyport. His susceptible temperament was readily brought under its influence, and his ardour made him join in the extravagances which usually accompany revivals, and he believed himself truly converted, but when he got back to college, where scepticism was so generally prevalent that even sober religion was scoffed at as belonging to a bygone age, his excited feelings, instead of arousing sympathy, became only an object of ridicule. He had not the strength of character to sustain himself against the sneers of his companions, and his fervour gradually subsided into coldness and indifference. But the Calvinistic notions which he had imbibed with his mother's milk still retained their hold upon his mind.

He deemed himself a backslider, as one who, having tasted the heavenly gift, had fallen away to perdition, and that it was impossible for him to be renewed again to repentance. He believed fully in the irreversible decrees of the Almighty, and that he was one of those unfortunate beings who had been predestinated from all eternity to per-

ROBERT HALLOWELL GARDINER

By Harding

dition, a rare instance of a person construing those decrees against himself. He exerted himself, however, most strenuously, as he deemed it his duty by every means in his power to promote the cause of religion and virtue, though those exertions would be unavailing to turn from him the wrath of the Almighty. When Mr. Olney came to us in 1817, he became a very devoted instructor in the Sunday School and was indefatigable in his exertions to increase the attendance at Church and in the Sunday School.

Principally from his exertions, and the popularity of Mr. Olney, the number who enrolled themselves as parishioners on the parish book was doubled. I was induced to take Noyes into my employ, and as he did quite well while he was under my supervision, I intrusted him with the whole charge of my business while I was absent in Boston one winter. He was, I believe, honest, but when I came back in the spring, I found everything in confusion, nor was he ever able to render a consistent account on his transactions, or tell what had become of all the monies he had received from me during my absence. I reluctantly came into the belief that he was indulging in habits of intemperance, and felt it my duty to remonstrate with him upon the subject, but I could never get him to acknowledge the truth of what had become obvious to the whole community. To his general denial I brought instances of which he could not but acknowledge the truth, but some plausible excuse was always ready, that he had been wet, or exposed to the cold, and had taken a little spirit on an empty stomach, but he never allowed the habit. With all his faults he had so much warmth and disinterestedness of character that it was impossible not to feel an interest in him. I could no longer trust him as an agent, but Mr. Swan, with whom I was connected in business, readily assented to sending him out as supercargo to the West Indies in one of our vessels, with definite instructions, to which he promised to adhere. He took out an adventure on his own account of the value of $500.00. The money for it he had borrowed of a friend at Newburyport on my endorsement, which, of course, I had afterwards to pay.

The voyage was planned by Mr. Vaughan with great

judgment, and, if Noyes had carried out his instructions, would doubtless have yielded a handsome profit. But unhappily Noyes had no confidence in his own judgment, but was ready to be guided by whomever he consulted. At the port of his destination he was told of the high prices his cargo would bring at another island, and, regardless of his instructions, to this island he went, but the El Dorado was elsewhere. He followed the ignis fatuus till, on his arrival at Havanna, he found his golden prospects had vanished, and that the voyage could not be concluded but with heavy loss. The captain was taken sick and died of yellow fever. This increased Noyes' depression, caused by the misfortunes which had followed from not following his instructions. The vessel returned under the charge of the mate, and the second day out from Havanna Noyes was taken ill with yellow fever and became at once delirious. He, who was usually so decorous in conduct and attentive to all religious observances, became excessively profane, clothing himself with curses, and in this state plunged into the ocean and was seen no more. With all his failings we could not but regret his fate.

Our system for the education of our children was not uniform. They were sometimes sent abroad to the best schools the country afforded, irrespective of expense, and at other times we had private instructors in the house. A completely private education for boys is attended with great disadvantages by nurturing in them an undue self-estimate. In a large public school or in a college, where they come into fair competition with their equals and there is fair play and no favour, the character becomes invigorated and manly, the boy learns to make a due estimate of himself, and all conceit is generally done away. These advantages may be obtained without instruction at home being wholly dispensed with. In 1814 I took Moses Springer into my family to assist me in writing, and to give instruction to the younger children. He had good natural abilities, which he had improved without much assistance from teaching. In the following year I made him my agent to take charge of my business in the village. As I spent the winter in Boston, I necessarily allowed much responsibility to

Springer. He was capable, but he had other objects that were of more importance to him than my affairs. I found, according to his own entries in my books, that he had applied to his own use from monies collected for me an amount of between $4000. and $5000. which he had balanced by his own note. He subsequently bought into the paper mill when I was part owner, and it was for seven years under the firm of Springer, Moore & Co. When the mill was first built, I had engaged Wm. Savels to come down and carry it on. The mill was burnt within a year of its going into operation without insurance. It was rebuilt by monies advanced by Major Grant and myself. On the death of Savels the company was dissolved. We had received in the course of eleven years the money loaned by Grant and myself and the original capital with dividends equal to 375 per cent. In seven years under Springer's management we received no dividend, and only 75 per cent of our principal. Though this was owing principally to Springer's mismanagement, yet the introduction of machinery instead of hand labour had made the old method of paper making less profitable. Methodism occupied Springer's thoughts more than paper making, and upon a careful examination of the books, I found that a large amount of the floating capital of the concern had been loaned to various Methodist concerns, and the company had borrowed of banks at rates varying from 7½ to 8 per cent to raise the funds indispensable to the business. I had been forbearing to Springer, but when he prevented his wife from relinquishing her dower in some land for which I offered to pay its full value, I became provoked and sued him, attaching the hull of a vessel belonging to him. His brother in law came forward and claimed the vessel, which stood on the custom house books in his name. I replied that I should hold on to my attachment unless he, a member of the Methodist Society, and Springer, an ordained minister of the state, would testify that the sale was bona fide, and I heard no more of the claim. Springer took the benefit of the bankrupt act, and I received a dividend of five dollars for my claim of between $3000. and $4000. Springer was a local preacher among the Methodists, and from his activity and intelligence had made himself popular among them. He was advanced by them to several offices of trust, and his great object seemed to be to become a conspicuous and important member of that influential body. This should have made me more reserved in my confidence, and I should have kept a more vigilant eye upon him in managing my concerns. He soon got one clerk under him, and then a second, and regarded his own importance rather than prudence and economy in my business. He also employed my funds for his own purposes without my consent. It was only the younger children that had been under Springer's instruction.

CHAPTER 24

CHILDREN

Emma and Anne were sent to a school of a few select scholars kept by the Miss Buckminsters at Brookline. They were the sisters of the very distinguished clergyman who, at the age of nineteen, was made pastor of the Brattle St. Church, embracing a large portion of the wealth and talent of Boston. He was a man of great ability, but by overtaxing the mind and not giving the body its due exercise he was cut off in his 30th year, without leaving any memorial of his genius but a few sermons. His sisters were women of superior abilities, high principles, and cultivated tastes, and had a happy influence on the children entrusted to their care. A friendship was then formed between your sisters and the daughters of Richard Sullivan, which increased the intimacy that had previously existed between the families. Hallowell was at the same time at school at Dr. Packard's. In 1819 we invited Charles Packard, a son of the Doctor, to become a tutor in our family. He had just graduated at Bowdoin College with considerable reputation both as a scholar and an instructor, for he had spent his winter vacations in keeping school. He was a man of principle, but harsh and tyrannical in disposition and governed wholly by fear. Laughing, whispering, or what he considered indecorum, was punished by pulling a handful of hair from the boys' heads. Of course I should not have permitted this had I known it, but the boys had too much spirit to complain. They regarded him with detestation, and Hallowell cannot get over the feeling of dislike to this day.* He

*Note of R. H. G. 2nd.

All that is said of Charles Packard is true, and we all did hate him and I always wished for the day to come when I could be big enough to thrash him. But to do him justice I wish to say that he was a most thorough teacher, and that I learned more from him in the two years I was under his care and more thoroughly than at all other schools I ever attended. When he left, although I was not 12 years old I was well fitted for entering Harvard College, and this was more than could be said three years later.

became a lawyer and subsequently a Congregational clergyman, and he called here three or four years since to apologize for his harsh treatment of the boys, of whom he had charge. He had become sensible of his erroneous principles of government, and much regretted the course he had pursued, and which he attributed (and I have no doubt correctly) to ignorance, acting upon a naturally severe temperament. We invited our relations, Philip Dumaresq and Wm. Vaughan, to reside in our family in order to have the benefit of Packard's instruction, and Sanford Kingsbury came as a day scholar. The education that Philip received under Packard enabled him, upon going to sea, soon to become an officer, and he was looked up to as the first captain among those who sailed to China. Packard remained with us two years.

Our family had become so large, Mrs. Tudor and Louisa Lithgow being permanent additions, with a tutor and two or three boys invited to be with us under his tuition, that in 1820, when the census was taken, we returned, including the servants, the number of the family to be 22. We therefore determined to enlarge the house, in which there had been original defects. The front hall was very small, with a narrow winding staircase, which it required strong nerves to go down without fear of falling. The front remained the same, but one of the parlours was converted into a hall with a broad flight of easy steps. A large dining room with a piazza was added in the rear, with additional chambers. The front of the old house is still seen on one of the napkin rings.

After Mr. Packard left us, Tudor, and subsequently Frederic, went to a school kept by a Mr. Putnam at Andover. He was a severe disciplinarian but a good instructor, and he made the boys learn. A relative of his, and brought up under him in the strictest tenets of Calvinism, became a Roman priest and was for many years pastor of the Romish congregation at Whitefield. So frequent it is that in flying from one error men rush into the opposite extreme. At this time Mr. Cogswell opened a school at Round Hill, Northampton, upon the European plan, with a large corps of able men, mostly from Europe, as instructors. Mr.

Cogswell was a gentleman in his manners and feelings, had travelled much in Europe, and was desirous of establishing a higher mode of education than then existed in the country.

The place he selected for the school had great natural beauties, the grounds were extensive, and the garden filled with fine fruits. He wished his pupils to be gentlemen as well as scholars, but the boys were not sufficiently mature to understand these principles. They could not resist the practical joke, and would act like mischievous school boys, nor, though they knew that all the fruit was designed for them, could they be persuaded to let it ripen. Still, the manners of the school were more refined than was common, and the instruction excellent. The charges were high, but not sufficient to meet the great expenses. Mr. Bancroft, who commenced the establishment in partnership with Mr. Cogswell, finding it not likely to be profitable, withdrew from the concern, but remained as a salaried teacher, and eventually Mr. Cogswell was obliged to abandon his undertaking. Hallowell and Tudor were there, the former 2½ years, the latter six months, and reckoned them among their happy school days.

In 1824 Miss Peabody came into the family as an instructress to my younger daughters. Elizabeth Peabody had unbounded benevolence and had the reputation of possessing fine talents, but she belonged to the school of what were termed 'Transcendentalists'. Her thoughts were obscure and cloudy, but clothed in fine rounded phrases, and they were deemed by a large portion of her acquaintances as evidences of deep thought. She was wholly devoid of that common sense which is of more practical value than all the talents in the world. She had imbibed many of the fallacies of the day, and was for some time a member of a communist society in the neighborhood of Boston. Your grandmother, who always liked what was out of the common routine of life, was much pleased with her society, and she had seen life under such various phases, and her ideas were so out of the common, that she amused your mother, who was also attracted to her by her earnest desire to be universally useful. Her schemes, however, were never successful. She undertook to conduct a monthly periodical, and engaged one or two gentlemen to assist, but the articles were so beyond the comprehension of common mortals that it fell dead, after the second number, to the loss of the publishers. Our daughters did not greatly improve under her instructions, and the engagement was not renewed after the second winter. Tired of aiding her abortive schemes, but interested in her for her disinterested benevolence, some gentlemen subscribed and bought a small annuity sufficient for her purposes.

In 1825 Emma's health showed symptoms of failure, and we were induced to accept the kind offer of the Ticknors for her to accompany them to Washington, where they proposed to pass much of the winter. The journey, though very expensive, was attended with benefit to Emma's health, and gave her the opportunity of seeing advantageously many of our most distinguished public characters. From Washington Mr. Webster joined them in an excursion to Mr. Jefferson's at Monticello, which they enjoyed highly. In referring to past events Mr. Jefferson coloured them rather by his present feelings and sentiments than by the impression which those events produced at the time. Truthfulness was no part of Mr. Jefferson's character, nor can reliance be placed upon the statements made in his writings. Mr. Ticknor told me that on their return from Mr. Jefferson's they stopped at Baltimore, and in the evening agreed to write down the opinions they had formed of his character from their recent visit. These views of Mr. Jefferson formed by Mr. Webster got into print, and his daughter, Mrs. Coolidge, made a defense of her father by saying that these views were expressed long after the time they professed to have been formed, when party spirit and party bias had coloured those reminiscences and had given Mr. Webster an unfavorable impression which he had not really entertained at the time. It is a sufficient answer to say that Mr. Ticknor has the original minute signed by himself and Mr. Webster the day after leaving Monticello.

Your sister Delia had formed an acquaintance with Mr. George Jones at Newport, which ripened into affection, and they were married at Gardiner, Sept. 9, 1834. Her health was not good at the time of her marriage, but we thought a winter at the south, where her husband's property was situated, would probably restore her health. On their return in the early summer I could not but be struck with the hectic flush in her cheek. I consulted Dr. Jeffries about her. He examined her lungs very carefully and told me that he feared that disease in them had made so much progress that there was little hope of its being arrested, and that another voyage or journey would only tend to aggravate the complaint and would add greatly to her discomfort. I felt it my duty to communicate these views fully to my dear child. The shock was at first very great. Her prospects in life were brilliant. With a husband devoted to her, and all his family feeling strong affection for her, with his large fortune, her own personal beauty and very pleasing manners, all that this world can give seemed at her command. All these were to be exchanged for the prospect of an early tomb. The first day after I spoke to her she shut herself up and saw no one but her husband, but she soon became reconciled to the will of her Heavenly Father, and frequently expressed to me her thankfulness for my letting her know her real situation. We were then living in the cottage. Delia and her husband came down there, and Mrs. Jones and her daughters, and his sister Miss [Mrs.?] Campbell, took lodgings at Mr. Rufus Gay's, half a mile above, in order to be near. It was an inexpressible comfort to us to have Delia with us, to watch the growth of her Christian character and her gradual preparedness for her Heavenly Home. The sympathy and loving attention of so many devoted friends made her last days serenely comfortable, while, as she approached the termination of her course, she could look upon death not only without terror, but as the gate of everlasting happiness. She died on the 8th day of January 1836.

CHAPTER 25

THE CHURCH AT GARDINER

The only place of worship in the town at this time (1804) was the Episcopal church founded by my grandfather Dr. Silv. Gardiner. The church which he erected was not completed when the troubles of the revolution suspended all his operations for the improvement of the country. By his will, he directed that the church should be completed by his executors, at the expense of his estate, and he endowed it with a glebe lot of ten acres and an income of £28 sterling, of which £20 were chargeable on the Cobbossee Contee estate, and £8 on the Worromontogus tract in Pittston, which I now pay. The completion of the church was not commenced till after my father's return from England as a permanent resident, and it was not completed in the year 1794, when Henry McCausland, a man of naturally weak mind, and who had become deranged by attending religious meetings conducted by fanatics, imagined that in a vision he had seen the Almighty dressed in a camlet cloak, and who commanded him to make a burnt offering and a sacrifice. He interpreted the vision to mean that he should make a burnt offering of the church and a sacrifice of the minister. The first was readily accomplished by putting a coal of fire, which he had brought from home in his child's shoe, among some shavings in the unfinished building, and covering them with a door lest the fire should be discovered in time to be extinguished. When arrested and taken before a magistrate, he related his vision, but without naming what was to be his sacrifice. He was deemed to be insane, and notwithstanding his dangerous propensities, was allowed to go at large.

The minister, Mr. Warren, boarded with Genl. Dearborn, whose determined character rendered the common people very much afraid of him.

McCausland, fearing to go near the General's house to

CHRIST CHURCH AT GARDINER

effect his purpose, took as a substitute a woman of the same name. He called at her house, but she had gone up the Cobbossee stream to visit a sick friend. He followed her in his canoe, and after the usual inquiries of the sick woman, suddenly snatched a knife from the table and cut Mrs. Warren's throat from ear to ear. He made no attempt to escape, or to deny what he had done. He was tried, but was acquitted on the ground of insanity, and remanded to jail where he lived more than 40 years. He wore his beard, then very unusual, and had a venerable appearance. Many persons visited him for curiosity, for whom he always prayed, using the Book of Common Prayer, and generally received a trifle of money in return. This he hoarded till it amounted to a considerable sum, which he finally gave to one of his sons. Many of his descendants are still living here, and are respectable citizens.

Mr. Warren was the first clergyman settled here. He was a man of small abilities and little education, unable to command the respect of the people.

He was succeeded in 1796 by Rev. James Bowers, a graduate of Harvard. Mr. Bowers had no deep views of religion, and was inclining towards Unitarianism. His sermons were merely pretty essays, and his very irritable temper prevented his having a beneficial influence on his people. In company his wife would touch some discordant string, and thus expose him, but in private they got on without much quarreling.

Meeting him, many years after he had left me, I asked him casually if either of his sons was going into the ministry. He replied with some asperity, that they should wheel a barrow first, and added that he had preached down every parish with which he had ever been connected. Notwithstanding these drawbacks, there was an openness of temper about him which made him friends, and having some little property in the neighborhood, he frequently came down in the summer for a few weeks, and when we were without a clergyman, preached for us, and he never left without receiving tokens of a friendly reminiscence in the way of clothes or money.

Rev. Sam'l Haskell became Rector of the Parish in 1803.

Tho' serious in his deportment, he commanded neither the respect nor affection of the people, and very rarely conversed with them on the subject of religion. It was during his ministry that my mind was relieved from the doubts as to the truths of Christianity which had so long troubled it.

The state of scepticism into which I had been thrown while at college had been a constant source of uneasiness to me, as nothing can be more uncongenial to the mind than doubt.

Being desirous of coming to some settled conclusion on this all important subject, I determined to read the best deistical works I could find, and see if I could obtain rest in unbelief. I began with Collins' Literal Scheme of Prophecy, and then with other works of the same character, but I found them less satisfactory than what I had read in favour of Christianity, and I turned to abler works than I had before read.

I studied Newton on the Prophecies, Butler's Analogy, one of the most profound and satisfactory works ever written, and Paley's works. Paley's Moral Philosophy is unsatisfactory from being founded on an erroneous basis, but his Natural Theology and Hora Paulina are very able works. My mind was at length relieved from doubt, and I became fully convinced that Jesus Christ came into the world as a propitiation for sin, and that the simple but sublime doctrines which he promulgated, briefly comprehended in love to God and love to man, would not only secure to his true disciples future blessedness, but a happiness in this life of which the wisest and greatest philosophers of the ancient world had but a slight conception. Mr. Haskell was not a man to whom I could open my mind, and after my marriage, when I told him that my wife and myself intended the next Sunday to remain and partake of the sacrament, he merely replied that he was glad to hear it.

In 1809 Mr. Haskell accepted an invitation to his old parish, Christ Church, Boston, and this church was shut up for a time. Residing in Pittston, when the weather was pleasant, I attended at the Congregational meeting house at that place, where Mr. Kendrick preached, whose manner and matter were so uninteresting, that I deliberated whether worship conducted with so little to engage the mind or the affections could be beneficial, but I concluded that upon the whole it was useful. The people collected with clean faces and clean clothes. They sat still and were serious, they heard scraps of scripture, and they sang hymns, many of them of an elevating character, and if their thoughts were not raised by the preacher to the contemplation of the attributes of their Creator and Redeemer, they yet received some vague notions of worship due to an invisible God.

There was at this time no other place of worship in this town but the church, and that being shut up, the people invited Mr. Humphrey to preach in the schoolhouse near the church. He was very popular with the Methodists, and as he seemed a well meaning man, and had no objections to the use of the liturgy, we invited him the next year to officiate in the church, expecting thereby that we should induce the Methodists to unite with us, but the Prayer book was a stumbling block to them, and not one of them came to church.

The following year Mr. Humphrey received deacon's orders, but he lost his Methodist friends without gaining friends in the Church, and having a large and shiftless family, he became indebted to everybody, and left at the end of the year. I then proposed to read the service, and as senior warden to call upon some one of the society to read a sermon while we were without a minister, an arrangement which was adopted.

After a time I found that the persons who were to read the sermon took no pains to prepare themselves. On one Sunday the person reading, Stephen Jewett, perceiving that he was making nonsense, exclaimed with a kind of grunt, "*Aye, aye, there is a leaf gone*". His manner was so ludicrous and unexpected that none could restrain a smile and some laughed aloud.

After this I took the whole service upon myself and continued it as long as we were without a clergyman, till the settlement of Mr. Olney in 1817. During the vacancy several clergymen came here and preached for 3 or 4 months at a time. Among them were the Rev. Dr. Leonard from Vermont, Rev. Calvin Wolcott, and Rev. E. W. P. Walls, but none of them received an invitation to the rectorship. When there was no clergyman here, and I could hear of any Congregational clergyman disengaged for the succeeding Sunday, I invited him to officiate for us. The invitation was generally accepted so far as to preach, but not being familiar with the prayer book they always chose that I should read the prayers. I conducted the service about three years and a half, and whatever might be the weather, I endeavoured to be at church so as to commence punctually at the stated time.*

If the weather was very stormy and only a few collected in the morning, the afternoon service was omitted. In fine weather and good walking we collected a congregation of from 50 to 60.

Small as the numbers were, the keeping up of the regular service was the means, I have no doubt, of preserving the church alive for better times.

By my grandfather's will, the legacy was to be paid by the legatee directly to the rector, and in case of vacancy, the accumulation was to be paid to his successor. After we had been several years without a rector, I proposed to the parish that the legacy and its accumulation should be applied to the erection of a parsonage, with the understanding that the succeeding rector should relinquish his claim to arrearages. This was adopted, and Nathan Bridge was appointed to prepare a plan, and to superintend the erection of the house, which is now occupied by Mr. Pratt. Bridge was a bachelor, and he did not plan a convenient

*Note of R. H. G. 2nd.

Among the clergy officiating during the vacancy previous to the rectorship of Mr. Olney, Rev. Mr. Wells is mentioned. This must be a mistake, as he was not ordained till long after this. He was a protege of Mrs. Nelson of Castine. She suggested to him that he should study for the ministry, then take the parish at Gardiner and marry Mr. Gardiner's eldest daughter. He attempted to carry out the full programme, but failed in the two latter points. He was popular in the parish, but towards the close of his year's trial the Duke of York died. On the Sunday after the news was received, in a long sermon he recounted in detail all the gorgeous funeral pomp. As the Duke of York was a very disreputable character, with nothing to recommend him but his being the son of George III and brother of George IV, this sermon settled the question and on Easter Monday he received scarcely a vote as Rector.

house. The rooms were too small, but I did not interfere, as I deemed it important that the parish should feel that everything was not under my control.

When Mr. Olney came here, I added the octagon room at my own expense.

I have mentioned that our Church was without any regular pastor from 1809, when Mr. Haskell left us, till 1817. During that time we had an annual visit of a couple of days from Bishop Griswold, and I endeavoured to impress upon him the difficulty of keeping our society alive, if it was much longer deprived of the regular administration of the ordinances of the Church. But the prejudices against the Church, on account of its clergy having generally adhered to the side of the Crown during the revolutionary troubles, had not wholly subsided, and young men were loth to prepare for a profession in which there seemed little prospect of their obtaining employment. At length, in the early part of 1817, Bishop Griswold wrote me that he had just ordained the Rev. G. W. Olney, who had expressed a willingness to officiate here, and he thought there was promise of his becoming a valuable clergyman. His mother belonged to one of the first families in Providence, but she had married below her station, and the education of their son had been wholly neglected. He had been as a lad bound apprentice to a baker, and while in that situation was a constant attendant at the theatre, where he acquired the art of modulating a naturally fine voice. He also became deeply impressed with the truth of religion, and having great sensibility, he determined at once to devote himself to its service and commenced his studies under Bishop Griswold. We were in constant expectation during the whole summer, after the reception of the Bishop's letter, of seeing him here, but he stopped on his way to preach both at Portsmouth and Portland, where he was greatly admired. At Portsmouth it was on the invitation of Dr. Burroughs, who was to be absent on a journey for a number of weeks, and at Portland, where the Church had been shut up for several years, at the invitation of the wardens. At the former place, the ladies testified their approbation by presenting him with a trunk filled with handsome clothes, and at the latter place, by the daughter of one of the richest merchants promising him her hand. It was autumn, therefore, before he reached Gardiner. I at once invited him to make our house his home and gave up my library for his study. Mr. Olney was soon after instituted, the Rev. Dr. Burroughs preaching on the occasion.

The fame of Mr. O's preaching preceded him, and our little church would not hold the numbers desirous of hearing him. His preaching was fervent and exciting, and he obtained great power over his hearers. Some few persons who remembered Whitefield said they were reminded of him by Mr. Olney. Both were gifted with fine voices which attendance at the theatre had taught them how to cultivate. Both were men of great sensibility, and had the power of exciting the sympathy of their hearers. Whitefield's eloquence proceeded from a heart deeply impressed with man's sinfulness, and with the mercy and goodness of God, and was enduring. Mr. Olney's feelings were equally vivid at the time, but they wanted depth, and when the early fervour of his religion had subsided, his thoughts were gradually drawn away from religion by a worldly wife. His eloquence then forsook him, and the same sermons which were delivered with deep emotion when he first came here, and drew tears from crowded audiences, when repeated some years afterwards in an unanimated voice fell lifeless upon an inattentive audience. In the early part of his ministry Mr. Olney acquired great influence over a number of young persons, whose religious character was improved by it. Among them were Louisa Lithgow, an inmate in our house, Harriet Merrick (Mrs. John A. Vaughan), who staid much with us, and Elizabeth Gardiner, who remained with us while her parents were absent in Europe. It required a firmer character than Mr. Olney's not to be unfavorably affected by his excessive popularity, and by the crowds that followed his preaching.

Self indulgence followed the incense offered him, and he learnt to consider his own comfort and convenience rather than that of others. During his winter's residence with us he several times spoke to me of the danger which a young clergyman's character would sustain by marrying a woman engaged in the fashionable frivolities of the day, and scarcely bestowing a thought upon the other world to which we were all hastening. I, of course, fully agreed with him, but as he seemed fully aware of his danger, I did not think it necessary to say, 'Why, then, do you marry Miss Clap, who you know can never sympathize with your pursuits but will be ever enticing you away from your duties and making them distasteful to you?' Notwithstanding, he married in the spring Miss Clap, the daughter of an uneducated man who had made a large fortune as a sea captain. She had been fascinated by his eloquence and by his power of attracting crowds to hear him, but she had not a single quality to fit her for the duties of a clergyman's wife. As the contracted rooms of the parsonage would appear forbidding to the daughter of a wealthy merchant living in a large house, in order to make the residence more attractive, I added at my own expense a large oval room in the front.

During the winter I showed Mr. Olney an article in the London Christian Observer upon the benefits of the cause of religion that had been derived from the establishment of Sunday schools. He was much struck with it, and proposed that we should commence one here, and asked me if I would undertake it. I replied yes, but that I must have time to reflect upon it previously. He said that that was of no consequence, and he gave notice at church, notwithstanding my remonstrance, that a Sunday school would be opened on the following Sunday, which was the first established in this part of the country, and of which I took the superintendence for many years.

The old church was much too small to hold the numbers who pressed to hear Mr. Olney preach, and the following spring the parish voted to build a new church.

I had offered to give any of my lots that the parish might select for its location. Dr. Jarvis, who had a fine taste and had given much attention to architecture, when he heard we were going to build, drew a plan that he thought would be acceptable, and which was adopted upon a reduced scale. An estimate was made of the cost of the church, to be built of stone agreeably to the plan of Dr. Jarvis, and as the parish was reluctant to involve themselves in debt, I engaged to take the pews at their appraisement, complete the church, and pay all the bills, provided persons would come forward and purchase pews to the amount of $8000. This condition was not fulfilled. The whole sales, including premium for choice, only amounted to $5025.84, and of this sum $1210. were never paid, making all that I ever received for the sale of pews $3815.84. Notwithstanding this, my feelings were embarked in the undertaking, and I persevered. The first cost of the church was $14,171.47. The small organ now in the lecture room cost $400., making $14,571.47. After deducting the amount received from the sale of pews, the net balance paid by me was $10,755.63. The bell was paid for by the sale of the old church building for a town house. I immediately made arrangements for the building, and I employed men during the autumn to quarry stone on a ledge on Litchfield Neck, near the bank of the Cobbossee Contee, which was to be boated down to the upper mills, and there hauled to the spot where it was wanted. I had a large boat built, moved by horses on the plan of the horse ferry boats, to bring down the stone. There was one rapid to be ascended, which was managed in an ingenious manner. The end of a rope which went round the shaft was carried ashore and fastened to a tree above the boat, and as the current moved the paddle wheels, the rope was wound round the shaft, and the boat was thus taken up against the current by the current itself. The foundation stone was laid in June, 1819. Mr. Olney stood high in the honors of free masonry, and several of the members of our society held their degrees in the craft and were desirous of the honor of laying the corner stone. I never had any respect for the institution. It always appeared to me to consist principally of ceremonies in themselves childish, and that the objects of benevolence which they professed were more fully provided for by the principles of the Gospel, and that a large portion of the funds they collected, ostensibly for charity, were wasted in ostentatious display. As the society is numerous and influential, many join it whose interest in it consists in the power they obtain of operating upon the minds of their fellow masons.

I did not accept the offer of their services in laying

the corner stone, which I was afterwards satisfied it would have been good policy to have done, as it would have gratified a considerable number of the members of the society.

Mr. Olney offered prayers at the laying of the corner stone, and I myself made a short address. Besides many of the parish, Mr. Tyng, reporter of the Supreme Court of Massachusetts, who was staying with me at the time and who was a strong Churchman, attended on the occasion. The church was not expected to be completed till the following year, and it was scarcely completed on the 20th of October, the time fixed for the consecration, though the joiners of the neighbouring towns had been engaged and, by the offer of additional wages, worked till late in the evening.

There had been a very severe and unusual drought in the summer of 1820. Fires had raged very generally in the woods and, in the county of Washington, had extended to the villages, and communicated to dwelling houses, which were burnt. Some vessels on the stocks were consumed, and two or three sailing vessels, caught aground. A drizzling rain commenced on Friday evening with the wind at s. east. The next morning the wind shifted to north east, and the rain poured down in torrents without any abatement till Monday noon, when the rain slackened. On Tuesday the 19th all the rivers in Maine poured down their waters with irresistible force. Every bridge and dam on the Saco, the Androscoggin, and Sandy River was swept away, as were some on the Kennebec. Bishop Griswold was coming to the consecration in a chaise with the Rev. Dr. Morse of Newburyport. On arriving at Brunswick they found it impossible to get across the Androscoggin there, and proceeded up the river to Lewiston, where the bridge was yet standing, but while resting their horse and getting their dinner on this side of the river, that bridge also yielded to the force of the current. The road this side Bowman's Point was several feet under water, and we had to have a ferry boat to bring our friends from Hallowell by the low ground. Notwithstanding these unfavorable circumstances, the consecration services passed off very pleasantly. Seven clergymen were present beside the

Bishop, who delivered an admirable discourse to a well filled house and attentive audience.

The consecration of the church was the acme of Mr. Olney's popularity. As he had been brought by a sudden conversion from a total disregard of religion to a deep feeling of its truth, it was not surprising that he should take a strict view of its requirements, and that he should consider sinful those amusements and recreations, particularly dancing, which, by a large portion of the Christian world, are not deemed inconsistent with their Christian profession. In the following winter some young people of the place proposed getting up a ball. Two excitable young men, who had become serious under his preaching during the short time that he was at Portsmouth, had followed him here and established themselves in business in order to enjoy the benefits of his pastoral care. One of them, notwithstanding, consented to be a manager of this ball. As soon as Mr. Olney heard of it, he sent for him and remonstrated with him most earnestly. He was apparently deeply affected, expressed great contrition, and yet the next day yielded to the importunities of his friends and acted as manager of the forbidden ball.

He again repented, promised contrition, and was again forgiven. Not so with several of Mr. Olney's communicants who had attended this ball, who were at once forbidden from coming to the Communion. This high-handed act produced the greatest excitement in the parish.* I was spending the winter in Boston, and the following mail brought me letters from all the parties. I knew that Mr. Olney, however erroneous and injudicious, had acted from the dictates of

*Note of R. H. G. 2nd.

In addition to the excitement produced by Mr. Olney's excommunicating all who attended the ball, was his course upon the death of Mary Tilton. She was a young lady highly esteemed in the parish, sister of Mrs. Frere, Mrs. John T. Moore's mother, who had been brought into the Church under the preaching of Mr. Olney. She died, and the day was appointed for the funeral. Mrs. Olney announced that on the evening of that day her sister was to be married in Portland to Justice Woodbury, and funeral or no funeral she must attend the wedding and Mr. Olney too. The only way of reaching Portland was by the stage which left at 8 A. M. The funeral therefore took place at 6 o'clock in the morning. Probably the feeling caused by this incident caused as great a shock to the Parish as Mr. Olney's course as to the ball.

conscience, and I knew also that he had very exalted notions of the priestly office. I felt also that the people had been very harshly treated, but I did not see how my interference at a distance from the parties could be of any service, and I did not attempt it. Most of those whom Mr. Olney had anathematised left the church. Some of them returned under other administration, but not to communion. One, the head of a family, who had been baptized by Mr. Olney and had been one of his admirers, has never since entered any place of worship excepting to attend a funeral. If Mr. Olney's religious feelings had not become deadened, he might still have retained admirers, but the fears he had expressed to me of the effect his marriage would produce on his character were beginning to be realized. His wife induced him to make frequent visits with her to her family, who were all irreligious people. Gradually the services of the sanctuary became distasteful. He shortened them upon the plea of weakness, and he has called upon me to read the lessons for him, when from my own feeble health I was less able to do it than himself. He wrote scarcely any new sermons, and those which he had once delivered to eager and attentive audiences were now preached in a cold, lifeless manner to a few inattentive hearers. It was difficult to realize that the same preacher was delivering the same sermons that had once produced such powerful effects.

He was aware of the trammels that were thrown around him, but he had not the force of character to throw them off.

Dining once at my table with a few friends, he said, with some bitterness, that a man's character depended wholly upon his wife. In the spring of 1825, he informed me that he felt constrained to relinquish the rectorship of the parish, and seemed disappointed that I expressed neither surprise nor regret. In the three first years of his ministry he had quadrupled both the attendance and the numbers who had signed the parish books as evidence of membership. When he left, the parish had dwindled down to nearly the small number belonging to it when he came here. I am not aware that he ever entered a pulpit after leaving Gardiner. His views had so changed that he, who had deemed it his duty to excommunicate his parishioners for attending a ball, hesitated not to play the violin for a party to dance on Christmas evening at his father in law's in Portland, and, when on a visit to Washington, attending a ball on Saturday evening and remaining till the evening had faded away into the Sabbath morning. He removed to a farm in Scarborough given to him by Mr. Clap. He there had a severe illness, brought on by intemperate habits. Rev. Mr. French, who was then settled at St. Stephen's, Portland, went out occasionally to see him, and was very desirous to know whether he was aware of the sinful course in which he was indulging, and whether, in neglecting the observance of his religious profession, he had at the same time hardened himself into a disbelief of the truths of Revelation. But his wife was determined that the state of his mind should remain unknown to the world, and always prevented Mr. French from having any private conversation with her husband. In that state he died, a warning to those who do not resist temptation on its first approach.

In 1820, when Maine was separated from Massachusetts and formed into a distinct state, there were but two Episcopal churches in the district, the one here and the one in Portland. The latter had been long shut up, but had been revived, principally through the influence of Simon Greenleaf, a distinguished lawyer and subsequently professor in the Cambridge law school. The son of a Congregational clergyman, he had by study, and at a distance from the church services, become a warm Episcopalian.

He suggested that the Act separating Maine from Massachusetts dissolved also their ecclesiastical connection, and that, no longer belonging to the Diocese of Massachusetts, we should form a diocese of our own. We accordingly issued a notice for the Episcopal Churches in Maine to meet in Brunswick in the ensuing August. At that meeting the organization was made, and the pastors of the two churches, and Mr. Greenleaf and myself, as lay deputies, were chosen to present our claim to the General Convention to be admitted into union with the Church of the United States as the Diocese of Maine. There seemed something preposterous in our two feeble churches being admitted to an equal voice in the affairs of the Church with the numerous, rich, and powerful churches in the State of New York. Massachusetts, though she had previously chosen me as one of her deputies, did not object to our petition, and after some debate the Diocese was received into union, and we took our seats as deputies.

CHAPTER 26

THE GARDINER LYCEUM

We have been justly proud of the general diffusion of elementary instruction among the people of New England, so that it is rare to find a person who, besides being able to read and write, has not a tolerable knowledge of arithmetic. When, therefore, I wanted to employ in my business surveyors and mill wrights, I was surprised to find them wholly ignorant of the principles upon which their arts depended, so that when anything occurred out of the common routine, I found them utterly at a loss how to proceed. Our farmers were still less intelligent.

Agriculture is the basis of national prosperity, and agricultural societies had been from time to time organized to give stimulus to the pursuit, but they had all fallen into neglect. Our farmers, living remote from each other and rarely exchanging their views on the subject, had followed a routine which yielded something besides giving them food for their families. If the surplus would supply them with other necessaries, pay their taxes, and keep their buildings in repair, they were satisfied without inquiring whether the product of their labour should not have been much greater. After reflecting much upon the subject, I became impressed with the belief that an institution might be established which would put the acquisition of so much science as was requisite to make skilful mariners, millwrights and other mechanics, within the reach of all who wished to follow these branches of business. I communicated these views to a number of gentlemen of practical intelligence, who highly approved them, as was shown by their subsequently sending their sons to the Lyceum when it was established. Wishing the cooperation of my fellow citizens, I called a meeting and proposed the subject, which produced a hearty response. I proposed to give as an endowment 312 acres of land fronting on Kennebec River and valued at $3744., to which I subsequently added 122 acres adjoining, making a total of 434 acres valued at $5208. They proposed to erect the building to which I only contributed $100.

It was then determined to apply to the legislature for an act of incorporation, and also for pecuniary aid in carrying out the plan. As the petition states fully the objects in view, I insert it:—

"To the honorable the Senate and the honorable the House of Representatives of the State of Maine in Legislature assembled,

"The petition of the subscribers represents that a donation has been offered of land lying on Kennebec River estimated at $4000.00 for the purpose of establishing within said town a school for teaching mathematics, mechanics, navigation and these branches of natural philosophy and chemistry which are calculated to make scientific farmers and skillful mechanics.

"And whereas it is an object of very great importance to any state, but especially one possessing fine rivers and a fertile soil, numerous mill sites and a coast indented with many and capacious harbours, to a state rapidly increasing in commerce, agriculture and manufactures that its artizans should possess an education adapted to make them skilful and able to improve the advantages which nature had so lavishly bestowed upon them, and whereas the State of Maine is in possession of these numerous privileges, yet while she has liberally fostered her colleges for educating young men for the learned professions, and possesses numerous academies for preparing youth to enter those colleges, and for making useful schoolmasters, she has hitherto omitted to make provision for giving instruction to her seamen, her mechanics, and her farmers, upon whom the wealth and prosperity of the state mainly depend. The recent improvements in chemistry, which give the knowledge of barren and fertile soils, and the best mode of improving them, render the importance of a scientific education to her farmers much greater than at any former period.

"Your memorialists would further represent that they

consider the situation selected for this school extremely advantageous, from its central position in a populous neighborhood in a fertile country where provisions are abundant and cheap, where commerce is continually extending, and in a town possessing uncommonly fine mill sites and rapidly increasing in population. They would further represent that in addition to the donation above referred to, a sufficient sum has been subscribed for the erection of a convenient building for the above school, but as a considerable sum will be required for the purchase of instruments necessary for such a school, and as the fees of tuition in order to make the school generally useful must be much too low without the income of some permanent fund to give a comfortable support to a person adequate to the task of instruction, they must rely upon the patronage of the state for the power of carrying this plan into effect, notwithstanding the exertions that have already been made.

"They would therefore pray your honorable bodies to incorporate a school for the above purpose, with a body of seven trustees with the usual powers and privileges, to be called the 'Gardiner Lyceum', and to grant such aid as will enable the trustees to bring the school into immediate usefulness." Signed, R. H. Gardiner and 51 others.

The petition was so far granted that an act was passed incorporating the Trustees of the Gardiner Lyceum. This name had been chosen to distinguish the institution as distinct from a high school or college. The following year the other portion of the petition was so far granted as to appropriate $1000 for apparatus, and another $1000 for the support of the institution. The trustees named in the act were, besides myself, Peter Grant, Sanford Kingsbury, F. Allen, J. Stone and E. Swan. Mr. Allen almost immediately resigned, and Mr. Evans, who was very efficient in carrying out the objects of the institution, was elected in his place. The trustees were sensible that the aid granted by the legislature was inadequate to the wants of the institution, but believing that when it became known it could not fail to secure the public patronage, they determined to commence its operation, and in July 1822 elected Mr. Benjamin Hale, a tutor in Bowdoin College, as principal and lecturer in natural philosophy. Mr. Hale was admirably adapted to the situation. He was a man of great industry, of versatile powers of mind, great insight into character, and with a strong disposition to break thro' established routine when change offered improvement, and therefore entered warmly into a plan which, tho' novel, promised essential benefit to an important class of the community. He had the power of gaining the confidence and commanding the respect of young persons intrusted to his charge, for while he was earnest to give them high motives of action, he thought it better not to notice and punish trifling misdemeanors arising rather from boyishness than from bad disposition.

An address was prepared by myself stating the design of the institution, and printed and very widely circulated in the name of the trustees. Copies of the address were sent among others to the two ex Presidents Adams and Jefferson, from both of whom I received civil answers approving the plan.

In order to excite a more general interest in the Lyceum, an act of the legislature was obtained in 1823 establishing a board of visitors, having concurrent jurisdiction with the trustees in the government of the institution. It was to consist of 15 persons, of whom the governor, president of the Senate, and speaker of the house were to be ex officio members. The members, excepting those ex officio, were in the first instance to be appointed by the governor, and vacancies subsequently to be filled by the board itself. The appointments were made and accepted, and a highly respectable board continued to act as long as the institution continued in a flourishing condition. Several of them expressed their approbation by tokens of good will. A bell was presented by some gentlemen of Augusta, a share in the Saco Bank by Mr. Thurston of that place, and smaller donations from other persons. To carry out the plan of the institution other instructors were needed, and in 1824 Nathaniel Haines was chosen tutor. He was quite competent to the situation, but pulmonary disease had taken such firm hold of his constitution that after a few months he was obliged to relinquish the situation. A knowledge of chemistry, natural history and botany were embraced in the programme of the institution, and Dr. Ezekiel Holmes, a graduate of Bowdoin College, who had received a regular medical education, was engaged as instructor. With considerable attainments, he wanted order and method to make those attainments available to the students. The same want of order brought him in debt to every body. He borrowed money of every one who would lend him and so far from esteeming these loans as favors, he seemed to acquire a dislike to those of whom he had borrowed, even as in my own case, I had never asked for repayment. He never commanded the respect of the students, and I deemed it a very unfortunate circumstance for the institution that he had ever been connected with it.

As discipline is administered in literary institutions, the students are placed in a false position when an offense has been committed. They either must be guilty of falsehood by professing ignorance of what they perfectly well know, or else be guilty of what in their code of morality is a much graver offense—betraying a fellow student. Mr. Hale and myself thought that if discipline should be administered by the students themselves, these evils would be avoided, and order more perfectly preserved. We therefore drew up a system in imitation of courts of justice. The students were to elect all the officers but the judge who was to be the principal without other power than that of preserving order. Culprits were to be tried before juries of the students, who awarded the punishment to which those who were found guilty were to be subjected. There was also a double register kept of merits and demerits, one for lessons and one for conduct. The system worked well under Dr. Hale who entered into it, but his successor did not like the additional labour it caused, and under him it fell into disuse.

At the time the Lyceum was established several writers suggested in pamphlets and public prints that by uniting manual labor with school instruction the health of the boys would be increased, and the profits of their labour would defray all the expenses of their education. As our institution was more especially designed for the benefit of the labouring classes, it behooved us more especially to try a scheme which had the approbation of many philanthropists to recommend it. I accordingly fitted up a work shop with water power, and engaged a suitable superintendent to direct and oversee the boys' labour, for which they were to be paid. It is needless to say that the plan failed, for tho' it has been tried under every variety of organization, how could it be otherwise when an apprentice who devotes his whole time to the acquisition of the trade which is to be his future support, cannot earn his expenses during the first two years of his service?

The scholars at this time were so numerous that suitable boarding places could not be found for them. I was therefore induced to put up a boarding house for their accommodation containing 24 chambers with an L in the rear for the family. This building, exclusive of land, cost me $4571., and when the Lyceum was closed the building was sold for the materials to be taken down and brought but a trifle. It being thought desirable that agricultural experiments should be tried under Dr. Holmes, I gave the Lyceum a deed of 15 acres of excellent land within a quarter of a mile of the church but as the experiments were not tried, the land was reconveyed to me.

While the Lyceum was in its most flourishing condition and just before the second grant from the State of $1000 per annum, which had been made for three years, was about to expire, Mr. Hale was chosen professor of chemistry in Dartmouth College. He notified the trustees that he should accept the offered professional chair, and should resign his office of principal in the coming August, 1827. His loss was irreparable. He had identified himself with the institution, and associated its success with his own reputation. When Mr. Hale came here he was a licentiate in the congregational denomination, but he had become dissatisfied with their discipline. A case had recently occurred at Freeport, where the pastor and his pupils had come to a dead lock, the council chosen by each party deciding in favor of the party calling them. He here became acquainted with our beautiful liturgy, and studying the principles of church government became a very decided churchman. While he remained here, we were on the most intimate terms and always acted together, and I retained a strong friendship for him thro' life, which was heartily reciprocated.

The plan of the school required considerable funds for its support, and from the general approbation with which the plan was received by the public it was supposed that these funds would be readily granted by the legislature. It had however been but a short time in operation before jealousies were excited, and opposition grew up from various quarters. The academies found their scholars attracted to the superior education at the Lyceum and the colleges believed that they would lose scholars who could dispense with the classics and be satisfied with a more practical knowledge, attained with a less amount of time and money.

Then came into operation the religious prejudice. All the higher institutions of learning were under the patronage of some particular denomination. They therefore combined against an institution which claimed no sectarian support. The second grant of $1000 per annum was about expiring when Mr. Hale left, and from the determined opposition to its renewal it was evident that no further aid could be expected from the state. It would have been wise therefore to have at once said that, the state having refused to continue its expected aid, the trustees were obliged to close the institution. This was my own opinion, but the feeling of the citizens was so strong for its continuance that we elected Mr. Lathrop in Mr. Hale's place and when he was chosen to a western college, Mr. Luther Cushing. Both of these gentlemen were good scholars but neither of them felt that he had engaged in a business which was to continue for life, but looked forward to other professions.

The institution gradually languished till my advances to sustain it amounted, exclusive of any interest, to a sum of between $1200. and $1300., when I declined to make further advances and it was closed.

Since that period, the subject of affording scientific education to those not designed for the learned professions has attracted public attention. By the liberality of Abbot Lawrence the scientific school has been founded at Cambridge and has received ample endowment. Many of the colleges have modified their laws. Some admit students to practical courses, and others permit those who are not members of the college to attend particular courses of lectures. A higher practical education is therefore now afforded to those who desire it than could be attained at the Lyceum, which was only designed to give needful instruction to the labouring mechanic without raising him out of his position.

CHAPTER 27

REBUILDING OAKLANDS

The old house had been erected in 1810. In its construction I had taken pains against the risk of fire by having a separate flue and chimney to every fire place. Before the building was completed I saw that the garret was so large that a convenient room might be made in it and still leave room for stowing any things not in immediate use, and I had a fire place made in it. This also had its separate flue and chimney, which adjoined the kitchen chimney. This fire place was used by the servants for the reception of empty boxes, which were frequently put there with the paper or cotton used in packing them still remaining in them. On the morning of the 2d of November, 1834, at about 10 o'clock, just as I was going to the village, I was told the garret was on fire. I immediately rushed up stairs and as quickly determined that the fire had made too much progress to be arrested by any means at our command. 10 or 12 buckets of water would probably have extinguished the fire, but they could not be procured in season to be of use. The water for supplying the house is obtained from a spring more than a half a mile distant, through a ¾ inch pipe, and therefore runs slowly. If engines had been on the ground they could not have been filled. The river was too distant and there was but little water in the brook. I therefore directed all our efforts to saving the furniture, which was done without much damage, excepting no attempt was made to save what was in the garret. The liquors were all saved. There was a quantity of bottled cider, which I directed should be offered to the people who had come to assist, but by some blunder they gave them the eclipse wine instead, which they probably thought not half as good as whiskey.*

*Note of R. H. G. 2nd.

The 2nd of November 1834 snow was falling and father proposed to me after breakfast to burn the chimnies. The kitchen chimney

OAKLANDS

The kitchen chimney had been on fire, and I never doubted that ignited soot went up the kitchen [flue] and

was very foul and the soot burned vehemently, and no doubt the burning soot fell down the adjoining flue, and as there was no hearth in the garret fireplace it might have set fire to the flooring or as suggested to boxes.

After burning the chimnies father and I went to the village returning in time for dinner. He was then upon crutches from a sprained knee. He went to his room to dress for dinner, and being informed the house was on fire immediately went to the garret without giving an alarm. Seeing it was impossible to extinguish it with the means at hand he returned quickly to his room to save his papers. In the meantime Emma who was in her room dressing for dinner rushed down to me in the parlour, "Don't be alarmed, the house is on fire, the smoke is coming to my room, help me save the family pictures." Thus every one went to work calmly. Jimmy Horn rushed first to the stable and turned all the horses loose, then up stairs to save his chest and then came running to me saying, "Oh, Mr. Hallowell, your nice new English saddle is in the garret." People came from over the river, saying that they had seen the smoke for an hour, but supposed it was only some new invention for warming the house. Crowds came from the village. Every one thought of objects in his own like. Wharf the stone mason proposed to me to save the underpinning which was done. Haseltine who had erected the additions to the house said "those large columns in front cost a great deal of money, if you say so we can save them." They were saved. I remember seeing Sager at a chamber window with a large mirror in his hands, and he called to those underneath to catch it on a featherbed, or he would throw it back into the fire. It was saved whole. Nudd the cabinet maker insisted upon saving all the doors which were mostly of hard wood. Even many of the architraves and windows were saved. The only person who lost their presence of mind was Lucy who rushed to her room in the end of the house, and being stifled with smoke, William Tarbox, who in those days was very energetic at fires, crawled in upon the floor and rescued her. The house having been newly painted burned slowly, it being four hours before the walls fell in. The dinner which had just been dished was all saved and served up at Mr. Evans' house and eaten heartily at 6 o'clock. Even pans of milk were brought out undisturbed. When nothing else was to be done, Mr. Evans came to me and said 'show us where the wine cellar is.' I refused, saying better let everything burn than a scene of drunkenness. He then said he would guarantee order, and I took him to the parlour over the wine cellar. A hole was cut in the floor, and every bottle of wine and cider, and even empty bottles and oil flasks were safely deposited in the stable. I urged that the men who had been working so hard should have some cider but by a mistake, perhaps of mine, some of the Eclipse wine was taken. Everything in the garret was consumed. Summer clothes had been stowed there, and winter clothes not all brought down, and all Francis' and Anne's things were stored there and among them many precious relics and letters. One thing there that was burned excited the keenest regret, it was the famous broad cradle in which three generations had been rocked, and which the children had so often used in their plays on a rainy day. When settling with the insurance commissioner, he was told that he must put as high a value on this as possible, and the proceeds were invested by unanimous assent in a silver cup for Frank, the only grandson, with the date of the fire upon it.

fell down the garret flue and set fire to the rubbish in the fireplace. The house was insured for $4000. Mr. Evans was just shutting up his house and preparing to leave for Washington to take his seat in congress, and he kindly offered us his house for the winter, which I gladly accepted. I notified the tenant in the cottage that I should want it in the spring, and we moved into it before Mr. Evans returned from Washington, and there we remained seven years. The question then arose about rebuilding.

Your mother and I were rather disposed to put up a small house for summer residence and make Boston our principal residence, but our children were all desirous to have the house rebuilt. Few country residences had so many attractions as our place had at that time. My daughters had been educated in Boston, and had formed friendships with persons of the same age and station who were highly cultivated and with excellent principles. Some of them spent a portion of every summer with us. We had friends of our age who came to visit us, and we also saw most of the distinguished people passing thro' the state. No Episcopal clergyman came here without staying with us. So much was this the case that one of our chambers got the name of the 'minister's room'. An Unitarian society had been established in Hallowell, and as it was feeble some of the Boston clergy, in order to its encouragement, always visited it in the course of the season. They were all men of cultivated minds and refinement, and most of them had travelled abroad. I always invited them to dine. Our connexions at Hallowell and Judge Wilde's family added agreeably to our society.*

We therefore yielded to the wishes of our children and made this our residence. I did not intend that the house when completed should cost over $8,000 or $10,000. Capt. Gage from Hallowell came down to see me repeatedly to

*Note of R. H. G. 2nd.

Father speaks of Judge Wilde and family at Hallowell, as adding to the other attractions of Kennebec which induced the rebuilding of the house. This must be a mistake, as the house was not burned till 1834, and Judge Wilde upon the separation of Maine from Massachusetts in 1820 removed to Newburyport in order to retain his seat on the bench, and his house in Hallowell was sold eventually to Judge Emmons.

satisfy that from his own experience a house might be built cheaper of stone than of wood, and stone was fixed upon as the material. A moderate ground plan was proposed, but one wanted an addition here, and another an enlargement there, till the plan greatly exceeded that at first contemplated. Then, to give it some architectural appearance, Upjohn was consulted. He introduced the hammered stone and battlements, which have been the cause of endless trouble and expense ever since. The house cost eventually $33,000 instead of the utmost limit fixed of $10,000. Before it was habitable, I found that my receipts would not meet my expenditures, the work was stopped, and the house was shut up in its unfinished state and so remained till the State of Massachusetts relinquished to your grandfather Tudor's heirs some shares in the South Boston Association which had been pledged by him as security for his liability on a note of John Peck to the state. The dividends on the stock having paid up the debt and interest in full, the state relinquished the shares to the heirs, and your mother advanced enough of the proceeds to pay the expense of finishing enough of the house to make it habitable, and we moved in, the dining room still remaining unfinished. This was also completed two or three years afterwards, with a little aid from your mother.* (2)

*Note of R. H. G. 2nd.

At the time the house was burned, father was upon crutches, and being confined to the house more than usual, occupied himself in planning the new house. After the plans had been modified from time to time by suggestions of different members of the family, the present plan was adopted and a model made. The beautiful hall and stairs were entirely planned by mother, and I think the arrangements of the parlours opening into each other with folding doors. Towards the close of the winter, father went to Boston to put himself under charge of Hewett the bone doctor, who soon cured him. He took the model and plans of the house with him and inquired for an architect. He heard of Upjohn, an Englishman who was poor and supporting himself by carpenter work; the only job he had received as an architect was the fence around the common. The plans and model were given to Upjohn, and he was directed to give it an architectural appearance without any change of the general plan. He put in the turrets, battlements and buttresses, the hammered stone increasing the cost very much, and what certainly was a large and useless expense, arranged every course of the rough stone to be of a certain width and length.

CHAPTER 28

FINANCIAL LOSSES

I must now explain to my children how it has occurred, that, inheriting an ample fortune and with no disposition on the part of your mother or myself for extravagance, I should when past 50 find my debts had so accumulated as to force me to mortgage my property for their security, which mortgages still remain undischarged. When I came into possession the property yielded but a moderate income. The settlement with Silvester Whipple and with the squatters caused an expenditure of over $10,000, and in order to develope the natural advantages of the place I was induced to expend large sums in improvements. But business for the first 3 years and a half, till the commencement of the commercial restrictions, was very active. Village lots and farming lands were in demand and sold rapidly at good prices, which counterbalanced in a great degree my large expenses. I kept a set of books by double entry, and the yearly trial balance seemed satisfactory. My income appeared to be over $20,000. per annum and my family expenses never approached half that sum, so that my book keeping seemed to prove me in a very prosperous condition, and in my desire to advance the prosperity of the place I was ever ready to engage in any new business that promised success. I advanced the necessary capital for these concerns, and the agent for carrying them on, besides having a salary, was interested in the profits, but it is difficult to get suitable persons to leave their residences and their family connections to go into a new country to carry on a new business among strangers. The persons who engaged with me in these concerns brought excellent recommendations, but there was always some defect in the character which was kept out of sight and which marred the success of the undertaking.

The fulling mill, oakum mill, furnace, forge, nail factory, spike factory, pail factory, and other smaller concerns all proved failures, and the losses on several of them were heavy. But there was a great mistake made in my book keeping, which kept me for a long time from knowing the real state of my affairs. My dams and mills were constantly subject to heavy repairs, but instead of deducting the cost of those repairs from the rents and carrying the difference only to income, I charged the repairs to real estate, and as real estate was credited with all the sales of land, there was always a large balance in its favour, and the large amount expended every year for repairs was thus lost sight of, and it was not till the land sales were rapidly diminishing that the fallacy begun to show itself.

I have also been a great sufferer by fire. In 17 fires I have lost one or more buildings, and in several others have sustained partial injuries. Most of my buildings are classed by insurance offices as hazardous or extra hazardous. The best offices will not take risks in the latter on any terms, and charge very high premiums on the others, and as my buildings were a good deal scattered I calculated that the premiums saved would meet the losses.

Latterly I have had some insurance upon all my buildings but the extra hazardous. The total actual loss by fire, over and above insurance, will rather exceed $47000, but there was also a consequential loss, for the water power could earn nothing when it had no wheels to turn. All the mills on the north side of the stream on the lower dam were burnt, August 16, 1844. Origin of the fire not known, but conjectured to have been from a pipe or from boys playing with matches. A more serious fire occurred April 25, 1860, which burnt all the mills on the lower dam but the flour and grist mill, and many other buildings, but my loss was not so heavy, as many of the mills belonged to the occupants who hired the land on which they stood and the water power to carry them.

I have been a great sufferer by flood as well as by fire. Three times the stores on the great wharf have been swept by freshet, and the gravel on the wharf carried into the dock below, to be dredged up at great expense. The lower dam, built of wood in my father's time, was carried away, and the Swan dam was carried away from a defect in the apron. To prevent the reoccurrence of the same accident I rebuilt the dam with a stone apron, but a large log coming over broke an apron stone, and the dam shared the fate of its predecessor. In all these cases, besides the expense of rebuilding, there was a loss of nearly a year's mill rent of all the mills situate on the dam. The losses of my mills on the lower dam did not occur till after my embarrassments had taken place, but they were a great hindrance to my extrication. Till about 1832, I felt that my debts were not larger than I could readily discharge, but about that time my receipts from the sale of lands were rapidly diminished, and in the course of 3 or 4 years from that date, my extraordinary expenses exceeded $100,000. It is necessary to explain these expenditures more fully.

Anne was married to Francis in 1832. He was then in business with his brothers at Baring, but the business, not being successful, was relinquished, and your uncle Frederic made him a proposal to take charge of his ice business. The proposal was sufficiently liberal and was accepted, and Francis took a house at Fresh Pond in order to be near the winter scene of operations. The connexion continued but a short time. Without entering into particulars it is sufficient to say that your uncle has had a great variety of agents, several of them men of capacity and standing in the community, but they have all found the connexion too intolerable to be borne for any great length of time, nor have those agencies been closed with the liberality that the agents were given to expect. No other prospect of business opening, Francis went to England with his wife and child. The Company of Springer, Moore & Co., had just been dissolved, and the other partners were very desirous that I should buy their shares of the paper mill, which they offered on very advantageous terms. I immediately wrote to Francis that if nothing better offered, and he would like to carry on the business of paper making, I would buy the whole concern and put the mill in good order, for which he should pay me a fair rent if the business would allow it, otherwise it should not be exacted. He accepted my proposal, and I at once proceeded to perform my part of the engagement. Machinery was just beginning to supersede hand labour in the manufacture of paper, and it was important to ascertain what machinery should be adopted. For this purpose I sent Chadwick, a mill wright in my employ, to visit various paper mills and, after seeing their operation and obtaining information from the owners, to decide what it was best for me to adopt. Chadwick had acquired more knowledge of the principles of mechanics and hydraulics than is usual in labouring mill wrights, which made him very conceited. He was withal extremely sensitive, and not being treated with as much respect as he thought was due to him at the mills where the Foudrinier machines were used, he decided against them, and I put in the cylinder machines, which were afterwards taken out and used as rollers on the farm. The original paper mill when completed had cost $5500 and I had supposed that putting it in good repair with new machinery could not require an expenditure of more than $10,000. The actual cost, including the change of machinery, amounted to nearly $31,000, much more than the mill was worth.*

The next great item of expenditure was for your brother Hallowell. After his graduation at Cambridge in 1830 he was desirous of entering into some business for his support. He preferred establishing himself here where he would be among his family and friends. My assistance also could be more readily given here than elsewhere, and his business would tend to enhance the value of the family property. He

*Note of R. H. G. 2nd.

The mistakes of Chadwick in the rebuilding the paper mill is spoken of. The loss caused by Chadwick in this instance, though large, was comparatively nothing compared to other things. In the first place he introduced upon the lower dam a new water wheel, the wing wheel, and estimated the saving of water one half; he therefore estimated the rents of the dam which were $2,000 could be safely relied upon to yield $20,000 and the power of the other dams increased in like proportion. Then in the rebuilding of the mills after the first fire, a vast deal of money was unnecessarily wasted in the construction. Richard Clay a shrewd business man, one day observed to me in speaking of Chadwick, he has been a loss to your father of more than $50,000.

was led to believe that the manufacture of starch from potatoes could be made profitable, and after visiting some of the manufactories in New Hampshire which were carried on profitably, and ascertaining that this place possessed superior advantages for the manufacture, particularly in the cost of potatoes, which was the principal article of expenditure, he determined to establish the business here and engaged an excellent foreman to take charge of the business. His calculation was based upon the supposition that the average price of potatoes would remain the same that it had been for many years, 12½ cents a bushel, but his works had not been in operation more than 2 or 3 years before the shipment of potatoes to states less favorable to its growth commenced and rapidly increased, and the price of potatoes increased with the demand. At 16 cents a bushel starch could be manufactured at a small profit, but the price soon rose to a quarter of a dollar, below which it has never since been, and the manufacture had to be abandoned.* In common cases the price of a product rises in proportion to the cost of its production, but it was found that the starch could be as easily and cheaply made from Indian corn as from potatoes, and the manufacture was transferred to the western states. The starch business not being of sufficient importance, it was necessary to connect with it some other, and Hallowell determined to go into the lumbering business. As that peculiarly needs experience, it was desirable to find a suitable partner, and Mr. Tobey was recommended as a man of prudence and capacity and thoroughly acquainted with the business, and Hallowell formed a copartnership with him under the firm of Tobey and Gardiner. The selection of Tobey was most unfortunate. He was a good natured, well meaning man, but not a man of good judgment or decision of character. He was flattered with having formed a business connexion with Hallowell. Instead of checking Hallowell's disposition to

*Note of R. H. G. 2nd.

The first idea of manufacturing starch was suggested by Mr. Patrick T. Jackson. At that time potatoes were abundant at 12½ cts. and starch at 8 cts. a lb. After the erection of the mill, shipping to Mobile Charleston, etc. raised the price of potatoes; at the same time the price of starch fell one-half by the introduction of cornstarch.

engage in large adventures before the results of the first were known, he encouraged him in them. If they were successful he received half the profits. If they turned out otherwise he could meet no share of the loss. They shipped lumber extensively to Boston without being aware that the difference of survey at the two places much more than absorbed all their large nominal profits. We were spending the winter in Philadelphia when Hallowell made his appearance very unexpectedly to tell me that Bowers of Boston, to whom most of their cargoes of lumber had been consigned, had failed, and his acceptances of their drafts had come back protested, which they had no means of paying. At the same time he had an ulcerated sore throat. I was on his paper only to a small amount, but I knew that their credit was due to his being my son, and the unhappiness that would follow if I allowed him to have all his future energies weighed down with a load of debt which he could have no hope of ever being able to discharge. I therefore told him at once that I would meet his liabilities, and having kept him with us till his throat had got well, I sent him back, a much happier man than he came. Besides his lumbering operations, he could not wholly refrain from the speculating mania which was then universal, altho' I checked him as much as possible. There seemed to be no business done in the country but buying and selling townships supposed to contain incalculable quantities of the finest timber, quarries of the finest granite, etc. Hallowell did not go very deep into these speculations, but they all proved unprofitable. At that period the hotels were crowded to suffocation. Stages in every direction were loaded down with passengers, and expresses going off from one place to another. When the bubble burst it was thought that, with one or two exceptions, the only persons who had not sunk money were the hotel and stable keepers and stage proprietors.*

*Note of R. H. G. 2nd.
The land speculations referred to now seem almost incredible and can only be compared with the tulip speculation in Holland or Law's South Sea Bubble, and as stated almost never resulted fortunately. In the numerous suits in the U. S. Courts resulting from these speculations Judge Storey always took it for granted that there was fraud

Hallowell estimated that his assets would not meet his indebtedness by about $30,000, which I have no doubt was correct at the time, but, as usually happens in such cases, his assets for various causes did not turn out as well as was expected.

The third great item of expenditure was the rebuilding of this house.

The fourth great draft upon my means was from the rail road. I became a stockholder by a species of necessity. The Kennebec valley must have a rail road or be thrown back from the position in the state it had held for years, and it was supposed my property would be peculiarly benefitted by it. I therefore subscribed for stock to the amount of $10,000. Of this I paid $6000 in land, and was allowed $1800 for land damages, which, however, were expended in rebuilding my front wall and restoring to order what had been disturbed by the road. The road had been neither judiciously or economically managed. The funds raised by the sale of stock had been exhausted, as well as its power of borrowing. Extraordinary efforts were to be made or the road must be abandoned in its incomplete state. Preferred stock, guaranteeing 10 per cent interest, was created, of which I took $10,000, which has proved to be a total loss. Then the road must be extended to Waterville and Skowhegan, or a large portion of its business would be cut off

unless the contrary was proved. An instance, Henry Warren, brother of John C. Warren, visiting Bangor found it impossible to resist the prevailing mania. He paid $10,000 for a bond of a township. This he sold for $40,000 cash to a N. York Company, taking the precaution to say he knew nothing of the land and they must investigate for themselves. The company employed agents to explore the land. The original owner contrived to be employed as a guide. He took them on to one of the best timbered townships in the state, and the agents reported that the company had secured a large fortune, and the money was paid to Mr. Warren. In the winter teams and gangs of men were sent to cut the timber and it was discovered that their township was a barren worthless mountain. Mr. Warren was sued for fraud, and under Judge Storey's charge was obliged to refund the $40,000 and as general bankruptcy was prevailing he was ruined. During the height of this speculation father was urged to sell the lower dam. For a long time he refused, but at length he gave a bond to Sheldon & Evans to convey it for $200,000 and agreed if they made the sale to give them $10,000. Sheldon expected his brother-in-law Usher to take hold and sell it at an advance. Usher waited only to close up a large speculation in which he was engaged, but just then the bubble burst and the matter ended.

by the back route. Here again I was constrained to take stock to the amount of $5000. A question was raised as to the terms of subscription having been complied with by the corporation, and I was glad to compromise by paying $4000 and abandoning my stock.

Other losses also occurred. I had $4000 invested in the Steamer New England, which was lost by collision with a lumber loaded coaster. I not only lost my whole interest, but the owners of the steamer were sued as common carriers by the shippers of goods on board of her, and I had to pay nearly $400. in addition, as my share of the amounts recovered. There was a large amount of goods on board the New England when she was lost, but the liability of the owners as common carriers being a new question, on which legal opinion was divided, most of the shippers therefore waited for the result of the actions commenced before putting forth their claims, and when the suits were decided, their right of action had expired by lapse of time.

Another unprofitable outlay was in the steam boat wharf. There was no convenient landing place for the steamer, and with the promise of a handsome rent I built the wharf just above the mouth of the Cobbossee Contee. It was calculated that the current of the river striking where the wharf was to be built would always keep it clear from deposit. This was counteracted by the current of the Cobbossee, which met the current of the Kennebec at right angles, and the water continually grew shoaler, tho' it was dredged out twice at considerable expense. The wharf cost $3900, and after a time was abandoned by the steam boat, and since the bridge was built has yielded no income. A portion of the expenses here stated were subsequent to my being obliged to mortgage my property, but between 1833 and 1839, when the great revulsion in business took place, my extraordinary outlays exceeded $100,000.

I have thus given my children a simple statement of the circumstances which brought on my embarrassments, and from which I might have been able to extricate myself but for the very heavy losses sustained by the burning of my mills twice and the consequent loss of rents till they could be rebuilt. The most unfortunate expenditure was in the house, which besides costing more than $20,000. more than was intended, gave a false opinion of my property standing in the community, and involved a very considerable addition to the family expenses in order to keep up the establishment.

Your uncle Frederic and myself had been on the most intimate and friendly terms from my first acquaintance with the family till 1839, when my name on the back of his notes was no longer of the value that it had been once. In that year your mother in one of her letters to Mrs. George Lee mentioned that the idea of carrying ice to tropical climates originated with your uncle William and that Frederic adopted the idea from him, and had made it a most important branch of commerce. Mrs. Lee showed the letter to your uncle Frederic. He was extremely indignant, supposing that your mother wished to transfer to a favourite brother the merit of originating an important branch of business. He immediately wrote to me, demanding in the most peremptory manner if I was concerned in the attempt to deprive him of the honour due to him. I replied that I had always understood that your uncle William had first made the suggestion of carrying ice to warm climates, but that it was like many other schemes which, after being suggested, remain dormant for many years. That your uncle Wm had not the requisites for carrying any scheme into successful operation, and therefore that he might well claim the whole merit, as he had taken up a vague suggestion, and by much thought and perseverance had shown the fallacy of one of the received commercial dicta, that the nation whose imports exceeded in value its exports must be on the road to ruin. He shipped what was valueless here, and received in exchange sugar and other valuable produce of a tropical climate. New schemes have always difficulties to contend with. None had so great as this, and nothing but your uncle's indomitable perseverance could have brought it to a successful issue. Your uncle wrote me a most insulting reply, and that hereafter he could hold no intercourse with any of my family. This letter I did not,

GOLDEN WEDDING ANNIVERSARY JUNE 25, 1855

of course, answer. Two persons are necessary to a quarrel, and early in life I determined that I would not be one of them. If your uncle did not like my society, I would not force it upon him, nor would I reject any attempt to renewed intercourse. We have occasionally met since, and common civilities have passed between us.

After this date the family history is as well known to you as to myself. I do not therefore propose continuing this journal any further but will only explain the circumstances which led me to convey to Hallowell the grist mill. When Hallowell made his engagement with Fenwick, Mrs. Jones objected to the match without his having property of his own, that he might not be wholly dependent upon his wife's fortune. I consulted you all at that time, and as his happiness seemed to depend upon the completion of the engagement, it was, I believe, with the full concurrence of you all that I conveyed to him the most valuable and reliable property that I possessed. Mrs. Jones required also an obligation from me that the income from the mill should never fall below its then estimate. I gave the guaranty and the income fell off, but so far from Hallowell calling upon me to make it up, he has not only furnished his apartments in this house, but has furnished the library, and has from time to time replenished the cellar with choice liquors from his own establishment in Georgia, which otherwise would have been wholly exhausted.*

*Note of R. H. G. 2nd.

It was a most generous thing in father giving me the grist mill which then yielded $1000 a year and it was expected that this would increase, but owing to the cheaper production of the west, our people gave up raising their own breadstuffs, and the income of the grist mill fell off. To meet this change, the flour mill was built, and the old grist mill sold. The flour mill cost $20,000; value of water power added made total $26,000. The grist mill was sold for $2000, the value of the water $6,000, making the gift from father to me $8,000. From this was deducted the $5,000 he gave all his children upon reaching 21 years, and it leaves the amount given to me $3,000.

EPILOGUE

I cannot close this memoir without expressing the profound gratitude that I feel to my Heavenly Father for having blessed me with such a family. You have all shown the most devoted and affectionate attention to alleviate the suffering and add to the comfort of your aged and afflicted parent, nor has there been any difference between the natural stock and those who have been grafted in.

May each of you, when overtaken by sickness or old age, receive the same alleviation that I have received from you.

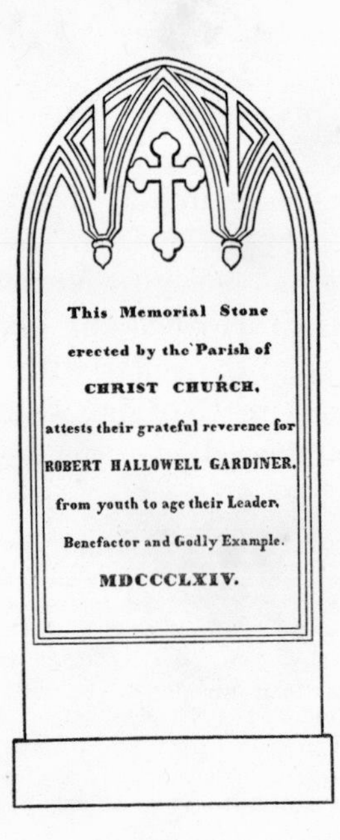

TABLET IN CHRIST CHURCH